ABORTION

Pro-Choice or Pro-Life?

THE AMERICAN UNIVERSITY PRESS PUBLIC POLICY SERIES

ABORTION

Pro-Choice or Pro-Life?

Gary Crum / Thelma McCormack

The American University Press

Copyright © 1992 by
The American University Press
4400 Massachusetts Avenue, N.W.
Anderson Lower Level
Washington, D.C. 20016

Distributed by arrangement with
National Book Network
4720 Boston Way
Lanham, MD 20706

3 Henrietta Street
London WC2E 8LU England

Library of Congress Cataloging-in-Publication Data

Abortion : Pro-choice or Pro-life? / Gary Crum, Thelma McCormack.
p.   cm.— (American University Press policy series)
Includes bibliographical references.
1. Abortion—Social aspects—United States.
2. Pro-choice movement—United States.
3. Pro-life movement—United States.
I. McCormack, Thelma.   II. Title.   III. Series.
HQ767.C743   1991   363.4' 6—dc20   91-35615 CIP

ISBN 1-879383-05-5 (cloth : alk. paper)
ISBN 1-879383-04-7 (pbk. : alk. paper)

 The paper used in this publication meets the minimum requirements of
American National Standard for Information Sciences—Permanence
of Paper for Printed Library Materials, ANSI Z39.48–1984.

Contents

Section One
Pro-Life

Section Two
Pro-Choice, Pro-Family, and Pro-Empowerment

Preface

The Pro-Life–Pro-Choice debate on abortion is the first volume in The American University Press Public Policy series on important controversial issues involving public policy. Forthcoming volumes will debate the pros and cons of affirmative action and the legalization of drugs. Books on other topics are currently under negotiation. The format for future volumes in the series may include rebuttals by each author of the other's position. In this volume, Crum and McCormack read each other's work and opted not to rebut.

Gary Crum, whose scholarly training is in the biological sciences, has been an active member of the pro-life movement since the mid-1970s. His position brooks no compromise. Abortion at any time in the life of the fetus and under any circumstances (e.g., rape or incest) is abhorrent. The mental or physical health of the mother and the physical status of the fetus notwithstanding, abortion is the willful taking of human life. Crum posits that in the abortion debate, the pro-life stance occupies the moral and ethical high ground.

Thelma McCormack, a sociologist active in the women's movement, assumes a more compromising position. Although strongly pro-choice, McCormack considers the age of the fetus (e.g., past the second trimester) and the mother's motivation (e.g., sex of the unborn baby) as legitimate bases for opposition to abortion. McCormack's section compares rules and practices across different countries, and the role and status of women in different societies and at different periods in time. It concludes that pro-choice enhances women's freedom and rights. She places the abortion issue in a wider context by comparing it to other political issues involving women's rights, such as suffrage, and sees both as means and ends whereby women become empowered to act as agents of social change. The pro-choice position on abortion is also part of other larger social movements, according to McCormack. It is aligned with movements that favor equality and liberation irrespective of specific issues because it places confidence in ordinary citizens to make important decisions about their lives and their futures.

Each author presents a strong, clearly argued, well-documented case. Some readers may change their minds as a result of reading both sides; others may become more convinced of the rightness of their original beliefs; and still others may acquire a new perspective as a result of reading this book.

Rita J. Simon
Series Editor

Biographical Summaries

Gary Crum holds two faculty appointments at George Washington University: a primary appointment in the School of Business and Public Management and a secondary appointment in the School of Medicine and Health Care Services. He teaches graduate-level courses in health management, health ethics, and administrative medicine, and he has numerous publications in those fields and in many other fields, including medical entomology and health systems strategic planning. He has held several health administration posts at the local and state level in addition to serving within the U.S. government as the director of the Office of Family Planning, Department of Health and Human Services (the "Title X" program).

He has been active in the pro-life movement for more than fifteen years, including serving as a vice-president of South Carolina Citizens for Life, president of Public Health Workers for Life, and director of the Castello Institute, a conservative bioethics and public policy center in Virginia.

Thelma McCormack is a professor of sociology at York University in Canada where she teaches courses in the sociology of health and illness, women's studies, communications, and political sociology. She is currently the director of a proposed graduate program in women's studies. A former president of the Canadian Sociology and Anthropology Association, she has been active in the feminist movement for the past fifteen years and was recently awarded an honorary degree from Mount Saint Vincent University in Halifax. Born in the United States, she did her graduate work at Columbia University and has been a visiting professor at the Hebrew University in Jerusalem, the University of Amsterdam, the University of

Western Ontario, and the University of British Columbia. Her recent publications include "Public Policies and Reproductive Technology: A Feminist Critique" in *Canadian Public Policy* XIV, No. 4; "The Censorship of Pornography: Catharsis or Learning?" in *American Journal of Orthopsychiatry;* and "Ethics and Human Reproduction: The Bias of Bioethics," in Don MacNiven (ed.), *Moral Expertise.* She is currently working on the contributions of women to the modern welfare state.

Section One

Pro-Life

Chapter 1

Introduction

It is difficult to find an issue more controversial and more politically intractable than induced abortion. It seems that virtually every newspaper has some mention of it and that virtually all health texts and ethics texts are giving the topic increasing print. No one can seriously say that the issue has been decided one way or the other or is likely soon to become an issue of the past.

Abortion involves not just one, but several knotty ethical and public policy dilemmas, including the complex epistemological dilemmas of deciding how we individually and collectively can determine the nature of human rights and of human existence itself. Right or wrong, many vexing social dilemmas are seen by large segments of the population to have their best answer in the *in utero* destruction of a human fetus, including the problems of child abuse, welfare support, and projected population dynamics. On the other hand, many problems are also exacerbated by more liberal abortion policies, including child abuse, welfare support, and projected population dynamics (the same list!).

Weighing these complex factors and reaching an effective, ethical conclusion for personal and societal action is not an easy task, and anyone who claims that it is probably is too ignorant of the facts to justify having an opinion.

The outline of this pro-life section of the text may at first seem to be confusing, but the various subtopics will be developed using what the reader hopefully will come to see as a logical train of thought—a train whose tracks will closely parallel those taken by this author as he has personally grappled with the abortion controversy. The format will be to travel from the most basic ethical arguments to the more complex, while

3

dealing with practical public policy options and ramifications at each stage of the journey.

This section of the book is based on the assumption that each individual biological member of *Homo sapiens* is equal in moral and legal worth to every other member of the species. The contrary, foundationally weak argument that subjective criteria must be used to label certain biological human beings as "subhuman" or "nonpersons" is examined in the latter portion of this section. As will be seen, subjective labeling of human beings is crucial for the pro-choice side if it is to argue effectively that the unborn have fewer human rights than do the born.

It is hoped that this text will permit the reader to examine these problems and delve systematically into their philosophical and public policy dimensions. One of the goals of this pro-life, anti-abortion view-point section is to be as candid in pointing out the weaknesses of the pro-life side as it is in pointing out the weaknesses of the other side. The conclusion, however, is that abortion is rarely (if ever) the best solution to the dilemmas that face us. In fact, abortion can be seen as having significant negatives when one dispassionately studies its immediate and long-range ramifications.

Admittedly, it is not easy to reach a dispassionate state of mind when reviewing abortion. Whether one feels that abortion is "the killing of innocent babies" or "a basic human liberty for women," there is little room available for compromise. The battle lines may swing back and forth in the public policy war, but neither a middle ground nor a relatively fire-free zone is very likely to appear, no matter how long the battle rages. To end the controversy, one side must be virtually banished from the field.

Eventually, everyone who considers himself or herself to be a consci-entious citizen must come to an opinion on this inflammatory issue, and then act upon that opinion, whatever that opinion may be. The issue involved is too basic, too crucial to the operation of a civilized society, to permit one to sit on the fence for long. At the same time, it is hoped that the reader who comes to this text with pro-choice sympathies will be willing to consider the pro-life position before he or she discounts its merits.

In the chapters that follow, the pro-life viewpoint is briefly outlined, beginning with a classification of the arguments for the acceptability of abortion. Then follows a step-by-step analysis of the key arguments using a framework that divides those arguments into what will be defined as teleological and deontological categories.

It is hoped that the reader will read closely the short discussion of moral philosophy that heads the next chapter. This discussion may seem at first to be off the subject, but if the issue of abortion is to become clearer to the reader, he or she must be willing to become more knowledgeable of philosophy, biology, economics, and a host of other disciplines. The issue of abortion has been difficult to solve and has been socially divisive, in part because it requires an understanding of complex concepts and facts. The reader must be willing to wade into these complexities or be resigned to hold a simple, catch-phrase-based position.

The arguments and opinions expressed in the pro-life section of this book are virtually all secular in nature and do not assume that the reader holds to a particular religious world view. However, in the appendix to this pro-life section some of the religious arguments against abortion, as found in three commonly held North American faith systems, are summarized for the reader who wishes to learn the theologically framed pro-life arguments.

One point that needs to be settled before analyzing the issue of abortion concerns the terms and phrases used to refer to the two sides and to the fetus. One side likes to be known as being *pro-life* and sometimes refers to the other side as being *anti-life* or *pro-abortion*, terms not accepted usually by the other side. Its opponents like to be called *pro-choice* or *abortion rights advocates* and sometimes refer to the other side as *anti-choice*. The use of rights-based terms and phrases for yourself, putting your group in the best possible light from a philosophical standpoint, is understandable. The use of carefully selected words has become a major part of the battle for the public's sympathy.

As a matter of courtesy and as a means of keeping the semantical smoke to a minimum, it is probably best to call a group by the name it prefers, not the name its opponents prefer. Certainly this is the best course when debating in the public arena—no matter how much you may feel that the people on the other side come short of living up to the name they have picked for themselves. Consequently, the terms *pro-life* and *pro-choice* are used to refer to the two sides.

In regard to the human fetus, the battle is similar, with the pro-choice side referring to the fetus as a *conceptus,* the *product of conception, the pregnancy,* etc. The pro-life side likes such terms as *baby, child,* and *preborn baby.* Here, the selection of pro-life terms cannot be compromised too much without telegraphing a concept that would itself mitigate the pro-life position's ethical conclusions. In the pro-life portion of this text, the following terms and phrases are used interchangeably: *the unborn, the unborn child, the preborn child,* and *the (human) fetus.* In accord with commonly accepted medical terminology, the phrase *human embryo* is reserved for the unborn child prior to the eighth week, when he or she becomes a human fetus. The word *baby,* perhaps the most emotional term in discussions of abortion, is not used alone or in tandem with the modifier *unborn.*

Finally, it should be clearly stated that there is no single, monolithic pro-life (or pro-choice) position, only some positions that are more likely to be encountered than others. It is fair to say, however, that the key pro-choice and pro-life groups in the United States and Canada, and throughout the rest of the world, tend to have a fairly uniform set of commonly encountered arguments. These are the arguments discussed here, with notes being made of any major internal disagreements in ethics or public policy that have surfaced on the pro-life side of the debate.

Chapter 2

Ethical Concepts and Common Abortion Arguments

P ro-choice and pro-life arguments can be grouped into the two primary categories of ethical thought, those that are based on *teleology* and those that are based on *deontology*.

Teleology refers to a class of moral philosophies that tend to look at the distant effects of actions—their good or bad consequences. Deontology refers to a class of moral philosophies that tend to claim that the consequences of actions are not the most important component in determining whether or not they are truly moral actions—the means used by the moral agent to achieve those consequences are equal or greater in importance.[1,2]

A simple way of expressing these differences is that teleologists say "the ends justify the means," whereas the deontologists say "the ends do not justify the means."

One of the most commonly mentioned teleological systems is that of utilitarianism. This 18th-century English philosophy invented by Jeremy Bentham (1748–1832) says that the best way to tell whether action *A* is more ethically correct than action *B* is to look at the results of the two actions. The result sought is the one that will produce the greatest amount of net pleasure for the greatest number of people. As Bentham wrote:

> An action then may be said to be comfortable to the principle of utility, or, for shortness sake, to utility (meaning with respect to the community at large), when the tendency it has to augment the happiness of the community is greater than any it has to diminish it.[3]

Another teleological system is hedonism, a system that evaluates actions based on their results. However, instead of using the more democratic "greatest amount of pleasure for the greatest number of people," it uses the more egotistically determined "greatest amount of pleasure for me."

Deontologists sometimes criticize these teleological systems as being too mathematical or cold insofar as the various means that are accepted (i.e., all means) to reach the desired "good" result. The deontologist criticizes the utilitarian, for instance, because he or she would allow a poor person to steal a small amount from a fabulously rich person if it were known that the rich person could never notice the theft or suffer from the loss. Also, the utilitarian might conceivably find himself or herself supporting slavery as long as the displeasures of those enslaved were more than made up for by the pleasures of those who were not enslaved (though some utilitarians would argue that slavery would never produce such a pleasurable net result).

Deontologists, unlike teleologists, speak of rights and of having moral duties to others. The argument against endorsing slavery could go like this: "Yes, a net increase in pleasure for society might result if we enslave some people, but that does not justify using a means that violates the right of each individual to personal liberty."

The utilitarian counters that the deontologist endorses a right to liberty only because the teleologist finds this pleasurable over other options he or she might have, and because the deontologist probably believes that the right to liberty makes people generally happier than under slavery policies. In other words, the utilitarian argues that the deontologist really speaks of rights and moral duties based on an underlying *utilitarian* motivation. The utilitarian considers words like *rights* and *moral duties* to have little or no meaning otherwise.

The reason for the discussion of this taxonomy of ethical thought is to help conceptualize the various arguments heard relating to the abortion debate. This conceptualization is helpful not only because it provides an organizational framework for a motley list of ethical claims concerning abortion, but also because in Western society deontological arguments are more likely to be considered stronger than teleological arguments. For example, a teleological argument relating to the abortion debate is that abortion has significant financial consequences for society. The pro-choice side sometimes argues that abortion decreases financial problems for society by decreasing the number of welfare-eligible babies. The pro-life side sometimes argues that abortion *produces* bad financial results for society by undercutting the demographic trends needed to maintain the Social Security system for the elderly (i.e., so far, abortion has resulted in more than 25 million dead fetuses—approximately 10 percent of the U.S. population and growing to a larger percentage each year. They would have paid billions of tax dollars from 1990 to 2035 had they been permitted to live).

The point will be made here that these teleological arguments are considered to be weak compared with the deontological arguments. The pro-choice side might argue as follows: "*Even if* we admit that abortion causes problems for Social Security and other welfare systems, that is still not enough of a reason to deny women their rights to basic liberties." The pro-life side would similarly counter with another deontological "trump" argument defending the right to life over dollars.

Common Bioethical Concepts

It is also helpful to review some of the key concepts often encountered in the field of bioethics, particularly the following: nonmaleficence, beneficence, justice, and autonomy.[4]

Nonmaleficence (do no harm) is one of the charges most basic to the medical profession and is tightly related to the pro-life position that no human being should harm another human being. The right to continue existing without being unjustifiably harmed is considered a basic right. One should not harm another person except under extreme circumstances, such as in self-defense.

Beneficence (do good) is a similar concept, but with an important difference. Although we might agree that I should not harm you, we might not agree that I should paint your house for you or give you one of my lungs if you need a transplant. Yes, it would be nice if I would, and maybe there is some unwritten social contract that we should pull together and help our neighbors, especially in times of trouble; but, in general, nonmaleficence is more of a legally enforceable concept in our society than is beneficence. A person should be given an award for being beneficent, but should be thrown in jail for being really maleficent.

The term *justice,* as used by bioethicists, usually refers to systems of social institutions that are ethically acceptable in how they treat members of that system: Are people treated the same in similar situations? Are the practices of institutions and authorities equitable, or is the system built on unethical principles that arbitrarily create elite and depressed classes of citizens?

The fourth concept often encountered in the field of bioethics is the right to self-determination: autonomy. Generally, that right is interpreted to mean that a person should be able to do and act as he or she pleases, as long as no undue risk is posed to others. A few personal decisions that pose no risk to society are not accepted by society, such as the right to decide to give yourself cocaine or, except in Nevada, the right to sell yourself into prostitution.

The right to autonomy, a key one in the abortion debate, has been embraced primarily by the pro-choice side. Each of the four concepts appears in the chapters to follow, but autonomy is addressed in the greatest detail.

It is of some interest to note that both sides in the abortion debate have chosen the strongest deontological, rights-based arguments for their names, showing that they recognize the power of this type of ethical claim: *Pro-choice,* for an autonomy rights argument; and *pro-life* for a nonmalef-icence, life rights argument. Neither side has named itself the *pro-finances* movement, for example, even though both sides embrace economically based teleological arguments as subsidiaries to their foundational deon-tological arguments.

Pro-Choice Teleological Arguments and the Pro-Life Response

Listed below are some commonly encountered results-oriented arguments for abortion and some typical pro-life responses. The list is not exhaustive, but it attempts to include the pro-choice arguments that present the greatest public policy challenges to the pro-life side (e.g., arguments about the life of the mother and about rape victims). Some additional pro-choice arguments of interest are also included, but, again, the list does not claim to be exhaustive.

The pro-life responses always eventually end with a deontological argument based on the right to life. As noted above, deontological arguments are stronger than teleological ones and usually can be ethically challenged only with another deontological argument.

It will be observed that even if the pro-life teleological arguments fail to overcome adequately the pro-choice teleological arguments listed below, the pro-life deontological argument will not fail in that task. It will become clear that to have a chance of overcoming the right-to-life argu-ment, the pro-choice argument must itself move to its stronger, deontolog-ical claim of the woman's right to autonomy or take a position that challenges the legitimacy of the pro-life deontological argument. Never-theless, it is important to learn the ins and outs of the teleological arguments because they are often encountered, especially in policy arenas where philosophical or theological arguments are often publicly, but not privately, down-played.

Pro-choice argument 1

Abortion saves money because it reduces welfare program costs. If it were not for abortion, more welfare-eligible babies would be born, thereby increasing tax costs. (This argument was discussed previously as an example of a teleological argument.) Besides, the world is suffering from overpopulation.

Pro-life response

Poverty is not a prerequisite for an abortion, so the proponents of this position might be assumed to be against all nonpoverty abortions. If they say they are for nonpoverty abortions too, then obviously this argument is not the key one—only a subsidiary argument that may be a smoke screen. (The key here is if the welfare argument were not true, would its proponents still be for abortion? Some pro-choice people would probably say yes, some no. There are people on the pro-choice side who are for abortion because they believe it will help to reduce the number of "unfit" people who reproduce.)

Another line of counter-argument might be as follows: Although immediate welfare costs might indeed be higher, the long-term costs to society are lower if the children are not aborted. The current loss of tax-earner support for the aging baby-boom population will mean that without massive taxes—or massive immigration of people younger than the average age seen in America—the Social Security system could be in grave danger of collapsing by the year 2050.

In the most recent year for which totals are available (1988), the Centers for Disease Control (CDC) noted that there were 1,371,285 abortions reported[5], or 352 abortions for every 1,000 live births. (The Alan Guttmacher Institute, which, unlike the CDC, obtains its figures on abortion directly from the providers of abortion services, gives a total number of abortions that is significantly higher.[6]) This high rate of loss of the next generation will cause extreme problems for the current generation's Social Security and Medicare support.

Ray Clinebelle has noted:

> Beginning in 1990, the 1.4 million abortions that depopulated the first age group each year over the past 17 years will result in 1.4 million fewer 17-

year-olds entering the 18- to 35-year-old age group. This is unavoidable. The result of this depopulation will be increasingly astronomical economic and tax revenue losses. . . . Continuing these losses for another 17 years, resulting in 48 million lost Americans, will severely injure this nation's socioeconomic system. Unless these losses are made up by immigration, there may not be a large enough work force to support our increasingly aged society.[7]

Daniel Callahan, noting the demographic trends currently developing in the United States, wrote in 1990:

The approximately 30 million people over the age of sixty-five, some 12 percent of the population, are projected to double within the next thirty years, to make up close to 20 percent of the population. The fastest-growing age group is those over the age of eighty-five, and their number could well triple over the same period. With that increase will come a growing demand for improved healthcare, bound to put a severe stress on the healthcare system.[8]

After all, 10 percent of the (potentially) current U.S. population has been aborted since abortion laws became more liberal in the 1960s (more than 25 million abortions against a projected 1990 U.S. population of 250,000,000). For the first time in the history of the United States, the people over 65 represent more than 20 percent of the total working-age population, and this percentage is projected to reach 50 percent by the year 2035.[9]

In looking at individual welfare babies and postulating an atypical scenario where a baby stayed on welfare until adulthood, Jacqueline Kasun has shown that the baby still would be expected to pay more taxes than he or she received from public funds, even after adjusting for the relative value of future dollars:

The stark figures prove that these tax payments will vastly exceed the cost of public assistance, even for those very rare children (no more than two out of a hundred) who spend their entire childhood on welfare. For the baby of a typical teenage welfare mother who spends less than three years on public assistance before becoming self-supporting . . . the present value in 1983 dollars of the expected future taxes paid by that child during his adult life is 3.6 times as great as the present value of the public assistance costs incurred on his behalf. In other words, the public assistance expenditures made on behalf of these dependent children are investments in human capital that promise high rates of return to the public over long periods of time.[10]

In regard to the overpopulation claim, it is necessary to define what is meant by overpopulation; the simplistic "too many people" is not an acceptable definition. Too many people for what?

Too many for the world's resources? We are not running out of room—the 5.3 billion people projected to be in the world in 1990 could easily fit into the area the size of San Bernadino County, California (20,064 square miles), and not even rub shoulders. Furthermore, some of the heaviest population densities in the world happen to be in some of the richest countries. Compare West Germany, with a projected 1990 population density at 626 people per square mile, Japan at 844, and the Netherlands at 931, with Pakistan at 335, Honduras at 117, and Mongolia at 3. Even in the United States, where the overall population density is admittedly only 68 people per square mile, the highest standards of living tend to be in the states where the most people are located (compare New York, with a population density of 365.5 per square mile and a per capita income of more than $20,500, with Arkansas, which has a population density of 46.2 and a per capita income of less than $13,000.[11] Another way of looking at the situation is to compare the current standard of living of the average American with the lower standard of living of the average American 200 years ago, or 100 years ago—even though the American population is higher now than it ever has been. Obviously, the claim of a likely correlation between standard of living or per capita income and population densities has no foundation.

Perhaps the overpopulation claim is that there are too many people for the world's natural resources and the health of the people dependent on those resources? Julian Simon, a professor at the University of Maryland, has studied this claim and has concluded as follows:

With respect to resources, all signs—going back in history as far as any evidence exists—show that resources have been getting more abundant and less scarce even as population has grown. In fact resources have become more abundant—lower in cost—because of population and income growth rather than despite it. Again and again, temporary scarcities induced by the growth of population and income have induced the search for solutions that when found have left us better off than if the scarcities had never arisen. . . .
In addition to the improving prospects for food and natural resources, the most important facts concern life and death: After life expectancy inched slowly upwards from the twenties to the thirties over the course of millennia, in the last two centuries it increased from the thirties to the seventies in the rich countries. In the poor countries life expectancy leaped upwards perhaps 13 years in the last three decades.[12]

A deontological argument relating to the welfare claims might be that, even if the short- *and* the long-term economic picture happened to support the claim that it would be good to kill millions of innocent persons, that does not mean that it is right. A person should not have his or her life snuffed out just because it saves the government or individuals some money. (The pro-choice deontological counter-counter-argument relating to personhood is discussed later.) Besides, if money is all that someone is worried about, kill the programs, not the children—at least give these human beings a fighting chance. Do not try to turn what began as a compassionate effort to meet the welfare needs of a depressed group into a cost-benefit argument to kill them—"saving" the money you just made them eligible to receive.

Finally, even if the world were overpopulated, it would be hard to conceptualize a future scenario so alarming that avoiding it would justify the current destruction of millions of human beings.

Pro-choice argument 2
Abortion reduces suffering by reducing the number of abused children.

Pro-life response
First, there is no evidence to support this commonly heard claim, and there is much evidence to support the opposite claim: "In the years following 1973, when abortion became legal in the United States due to the Supreme Court's *Roe v. Wade* decision, estimated numbers of child abuse cases have skyrocketed, from 167,000 in 1973 to 929,000 in 1982."[13] And Ney says, "Evidence suggests that acceptance of killing the fetus can lower resistance to abuse of born children."[14]

On another point, it is very difficult to tell which parents might be abusers. Even if it were possible to determine that a father will be an abuser, can we make the mother have an abortion? If the mother is a known child abuser, should we give her alone the special right to have an abortion? Should we not give the child government protection when we can tell there is a likely chance for abuse, rather than give the mother the right to the ultimate abuse (i.e., to kill the unborn child)? And if we cannot tell who is to be an abuser, how can we use this argument in setting public policy? And even if child abuse would be reduced by allowing parents to abort their babies, it does not mean that a baby is better off dead than abused. Does not society consider killing a baby even more unjust than abusing it? One should not harm another by denying him or her a right to life just because he or she might become a child abuse statistic—to rob someone of his or her right to continue living is the worst possible form of abuse.

Pro-choice argument 3

Abortion reduces suffering by reducing the number of poor families with too many mouths to feed. (The emphasis is now on the poor family, not society's needs.)

Pro-life response

Here we see where a poor family could benefit from family planning efforts and prefertilization birth-control methods such as condoms, spermicidal foams and creams, diaphragms, or natural family planning. As used here, natural family planning includes such state-of-the-art methods as the use of the woman's basal body temperature, not the calendar-only rhythm method.[15] Prefertilization birth-control methods are cheaper and safer than abortion and represent a more logical option than abortion for the husband and wife with limited means. (Some pro-lifers, in particular those in the Roman Catholic church, would for religious reasons eschew contraceptive techniques other than natural family planning. For more on the topic of Catholic ethics and abortion, see the appendix to this portion of the book.)

A more deontological counter-argument would be that once fertilization is complete, the family in poverty has two or three possible options: to redistribute already scarce resources toward more child-related expenditures; to place their child for adoption (there are long waiting lines for adoptable babies); or to place him or her in foster care for a period of time. These are not easy options, but they are better than robbing a child of his or her right to life just to save some trouble or money for the parents. One cannot be permitted to kill a child to keep from having to use the emotionally painful adoption option.

Pro choice argument 4

Women who are facing likely death if they carry a fetus to term should be allowed to have an abortion.

Pro-life response

Many pro-lifers would agree with this particular argument for abortion, but others would argue that it is a straw-man. Unless we are including situations where the human embryo cannot survive anyway (e.g., ectopic pregnancies—tubal pregnancies in which the embryo implants in a Fallo-pian tube before it reaches the womb, grows until it ruptures the tube and dies, and thus presents a severe risk of peritonitis to the mother), or unless we are including *any* increased risk to the mother's life, no matter how small, experts point out that death from carrying a child to term is never a likely conclusion. If "life of the mother" is meant to refer to cases where the mother's death will be imminent, the reference is an unrealistic one in light of today's medical environment. If by "increased risk" we mean a five percent chance of dying, or a ten percent chance, then we are only saying that death is still not likely to occur.

Perhaps it would be reasonable to define "threat to the life of the mother" as occurring when there is a 50 percent or greater chance that the woman will die if the child is not at least carried in the womb until he or she will have a 50 percent chance of surviving (e.g., use an induced premature delivery to prevent grave injury to the mother).

This definition illustrates a crucial aspect of the "life-of-the-mother" type of exception. The right to life is still considered what pro-lifers would call the paramount right of all rights—the abortion may be seen as a form of self-defense by the mother who is seeking to protect her own right to life. The pro-choice argument is itself a form of deontological, right-to-life argument, rather than a more teleological one. This is particularly a strong argument for an abortion, especially if the woman had no reasonable idea of the health risks posed by a pregnancy when she chose to take part in sexual intercourse. By taking a self-defense argument—a true right-to-life argument—the advocates of abortions to prevent the death of the mother end up on ground that many, perhaps *most,* pro-lifers find ethically acceptable.

Some important ethical problems still remain, however. The woman who asserts her right to strike out in self-defense against her own unborn child could be considered ethical, but the physician who performed the abortion probably would not be. Imagine the following, admittedly grisly, scenario:

> An ambulance comes upon the scene of an automobile accident where a man and a woman are trapped in a car that has hit a tree at high speed. The ambulance personnel see that both people are tightly enclosed in the twisted metal. The woman is in fairly good shape, with only a slight chance of dying; but the man is hemorrhaging badly and is obviously in need of immediate care. The problem is that the woman is trapped in the wreckage in such a way that she prevents

the ambulance personnel from helping the man. In order to get to the man with a minimum of delay, it is decided to kill the woman and remove her in pieces out of a small opening in the wreckage.

In effect, this is the ethical situation of a physician who aborts an unborn child that has a chance of surviving to help the mother avoid an increased chance of dying herself. In the car-wreck scenario, we might find some justification if the man himself would kill the woman to get the life-saving help he needed, but we find no justification for the ambulance personnel taking such a maleficent action against the woman. Because self-induced abortions are not currently legal, nor likely to be safe for the woman, this ethical problem prevents the self-defense argument from being totally convincing when deciding to abort.

This author's position is that the unborn child and the mother—and all human beings—should have their lives equally protected under the law, and that physicians should consider both mother and unborn child to be *bona fide* patients. If, as in the case of an acute ectopic pregnancy, the developing embryo/fetus is imminently doomed and the mother is facing grave risk to her life, then it seems ethically defensible for a physician to induce an abortion to save the mother's life. In other cases, neither the mother nor her unborn child should be denied a right to continue living.

Despite this purist position, however, the author does realize that polls show that a majority of people would permit a woman facing grave risk of death to have an abortion. If such situations are truly medical rarities or medical fictions, and if such an exception would not create a loophole that would eventually allow minor health risks to be used as excuses for abortions, a public policy allowing "life-of-the-mother" exceptions might have virtually the same effect as a national policy that allowed no abortions to save the life of the mother (as long as the child might have even a remote chance of survival).

Pro-choice argument 5
Women who are victims of rape should be allowed to abort even if abortion is not available to every woman on demand—to refuse them an abortion would cause them unnecessary suffering.

Pro-life response
Rape is perhaps the most difficult type of abortion to oppose, with the exception of abortions necessary to prevent the death of the mother. It

seems unkind in the extreme to say no to the woman who has been raped and who is seeking an abortion, especially if the rape and pregnancy have been reported in a timely manner to authorities. It is almost like asking her to perpetuate the crime for nine months more.

Nevertheless, even pro-choice advocates note that there would be an inconsistency in saying that the unborn child has a right to life except when that child's father was a rapist. Is the fetus a criminal? Rapists judged guilty in the courts are no longer put to death, so why should their completely innocent unborn children die? Therefore, the tensions between sympathies for the mother and sympathies for the mother's unborn son or daughter are in grave conflict—but it is another conflict where the unborn child's right to life seems stronger than even the right of the rapist's victim to have an abortion. By aborting the fetus, we only create another victim and encourage the mother to help limit the effects of her own victimization by victimizing her own child. The unborn child has already been abandoned, so to speak, by his or her father, but that is not a justification for the mother and society also to abandon him or her.

An often mentioned aspect of the rape-related abortion is that the mother did not voluntarily take part in the decision to have sexual intercourse. One train of pro-life arguments revolves around the fact that any fertile woman who has sexual intercourse, even with the use of contraceptives, has in effect chosen to take a chance of getting pregnant. There are no contraceptive techniques, other than surgical sterilization, that can guarantee that pregnancy will not result. Thus, by having sexual intercourse, the woman who would have an abortion if she gets pregnant has in effect played roulette with the possible life of her son or daughter. But in the case of rape, this aspect of denying an abortion does not apply, for the woman's autonomous actions did not lead to the pregnancy.

Still another facet of the rape-related abortion situation is related to the framework of the previous problem, where the abortion was postulated as being necessary to prevent the death of the mother. There it was seen that the threat to life held important moral weight whether or not the child was in the womb—the tensions between the child's right to life and the mother's right to life being so profound that they are used by even many pro-lifers to justify abortion as a form of self-defense. In applying the same type of logic to the argument about rape-related abortion, however, we do not see any justification for killing a born child because he or she was conceived by rape. The child is innocent of any crime, and he or she is not a life-threat to anyone, although he or she may be at least a temporary threat to the mother's psychological well-being.

As is mentioned in the appendix to this section, many people who feel abortion is wrong and should be outlawed nevertheless feel that abortion is acceptable if the mother was raped. It is easy to see the mother's dilemma, and not so easy to see the dilemma of the unborn child who has been abandoned by his or her father even before fertilization took place. We experience the mother's personality, but experience the unborn child only by use of sophisticated medical technologies. The mother is a victim of a terrible crime and she is requesting an abortion rather than expressing a willingness to carry the child to term. It is admittedly difficult to tell her no, even if we agree that the child is an innocent victim too.

For some pro-lifers, a legal exception for rape-related abortions is an acceptable public policy compromise, especially if the compromise originates and is fashioned in the political arena rather than in the "prophetic" ethical or theological institutions of society, such as church bodies, pro-life/pro-family pressure groups, etc. For this author even the heart-rending plea of the rape victim fails to justify the premeditated killing of an innocent human being. Nevertheless, it is realized that such a purist approach might be a difficult one for which to get society's endorsement. It is more likely, at least in the near future, that compromise public policy positions will permit rape-related abortions—even though such compromises will be logically inconsistent with the principles argued by both pro-choice and pro-life theorists.

One possible approach to help mitigate this potential inconsistency in public policy would be for society to underwrite a program whereby the woman who was pregnant by rape and who was required, or even who volunteered, to carry her child to term would receive from the government financial restitution, free psychological counseling, free prenatal care, and other appropriate assistance. This would at least make it clear that society was not completely unsympathetic to the rape victim's situation. It would also help ensure that any further victimization of the raped woman could be kept at the minimum level possible. Meanwhile, society would also be saying to the innocent unborn child—we will not execute you for your father's crime.

The case of rape represents a difficult one for the pro-life side to oppose with any fervor. In one way it is more justifiable than abortion to save the life of the mother, for in many cases the woman facing health risks knows of those risks before voluntarily engaging in sexual intercourse. The woman who has been raped may not have the support of the fairly strong "self-defense" argument, but she does have the strong argument related to the involuntary aspects of her difficult situation. A purist pro-life position would not permit a woman to have an abortion to protect her health or because she had been raped, but in reality even many pro-life people would vote for public policies that allowed abortion in these admittedly rare and extreme situations.

Pro-choice argument 6

Women and girls who are victims of an incestuous union should be allowed to abort even if abortion is not available to every woman on demand—to refuse them an abortion would cause them unnecessary suffering and cause a confusion of genetics and family relationships.

Pro-life response

Incest, such as when a father has sexual relations with a daughter, can be a devastating experience for the daughter and for the family as a whole. When a pregnancy results, the devastation is even more complete.

Incest-related abortions are special because of the family confusion that can result and the genetic risks to the offspring. A child born to a female impregnated by her father has a significantly greater chance of genetic abnormality, though abnormality is far from a foregone conclusion.[16]

It is true that a child born of a father and daughter union will have confused relationships—the child's paternal grandmother (the father's mother) will also be the child's maternal great-grandmother (the mother's grandmother), and so on. The child born to a brother and sister pregnancy would find that his or her father was also an uncle (the mother's brother). Although these types of confused relationships might be traumatic, it seems too harsh to suggest that they should be avoided by killing the child in the womb. The right to life of the child should not be denied for such a reason.

Another type of incestuous relationship might be the result of more distantly related unions between adults—say a 25-year-old sister living with a 25-year-old half brother, or a 40-year-old aunt living with a 22-year-old nephew—and might even at times be openly tolerated by authorities. Certainly no couple whom authorities allowed to continue in union should be granted any right to abort all their children because they were technically living in incest.

In fact, the incest argument, where it carries any strong ethical weight, is a subset of the rape argument. To allow an exception for rape would cover all of the pregnancies that resulted from forced or voluntary incest between adults and minors, or from voluntary incest between a minor and a minor. Even if the incest between an adult and a minor were voluntary, it would be statutory rape because the consent was given by someone too young to understand adequately the true nature of the situation where consent was given. Furthermore, women who are pregnant as a result of incestuous sexual encounters between consenting adults should not be "rewarded" with easier access to abortion.

Pro-choice argument 7
Abortion should be permitted in the case where fetal deformity will (or is likely to) result, because carrying the child to term will cause harm to the psychological health of the mother, will result in family strains, and will result in a low quality life for the child.

Pro-life response
The birth of a deformed child is a severely traumatic experience that all parents would like to avoid. If the deformities are profound, the expense of caring for or institutionalizing a child can be catastrophic to the average family. Even if deformities are less severe, the additional care needed for the child can still strain the financial and psychological resources of the mother and family.

The family strains, although severe, cannot justify the destruction of a human life. An abortion performed because having the child might psychologically harm the mother is less likely to be considered an ethical abortion than one performed to prevent the death of the mother. No self-defense argument is available, and even if the mother had no reason to suspect there was a higher chance of fetal deformity before she engaged in sexual relations, she would not be permitted to kill a born child who had deformities, so why would she be permitted to kill an unborn one? Two reasons sometimes mentioned are that she has a right to control her own body, and that the child is not a moral agent or "person" until born—reasons dealt with in a later chapter.

The most unusual aspect of the arguments for "fetal deformity" exceptions is the claim that abortion is best for the human fetus himself or herself. Here is what can be called a "euthanasia abortion"—killing the fetus for its own good. The argument is that the "quality of life" of the human fetus, if allowed to live, would be so low that the fetus himself or herself would want to be dead. This ethical situation is similar to a scenario where a person who is injured and paralyzed is "put out of his misery" by a well-intentioned friend.

Once again, this type of argument fails to stand against the test of what we would do to a born deformed baby, although some people have argued at times that the retarded and the deformed should be provided less care. In Nazi Germany during the late 1930s Hitler put into operation a euthanasia program aimed at defective children.[17] In general, people have not endorsed a lower level of compassion for born deformed children, and there is no reason to put deformed human fetuses into any other category. The deformed unborn child is not *prevented* by an abortion; the deformed child is only killed before it can be born.

Efforts truly aimed at preventing birth defects—such as genetic research to be used in genetic counseling before marriage—are ethical and should be encouraged. Amniocentesis and other prenatal genetic assessment techniques are *not* ethical, unless either abortion (the primary purpose of amniocentesis[18]) is considered to be ethical or the tests are likely to uncover treatable genetic defects. The morality of searching for unborn children to abort is like unto the morality of aborting those fetuses.

A final question related to fetal-deformity abortions mimics one of the dilemmas mentioned under the "life of the mother" arguments; namely, what likelihood of an adverse outcome is required for the abortion to be justified?

Under the discussion of the "life-of-the-mother" justification for abortions, we saw that defining the risk to the mother, whether the risk of death is 20 percent or 50 percent or some other figure, might be crucial for implementing any such rule. In the case of fetal deformity, what likelihood that deformity would be present is needed before abortion is justified? Would the slighter chance of fetal deformity raised by an incestuous union be enough justification? Would the risk posed by having German measles (rubella) during the most susceptible time of the pregnancy be sufficient justification? There is about a 50 percent chance of the fetus being infected with congenital rubella even if the mother is infected at the most sensitive time in the unborn child's development—around the eighth week. Even then "as many as ⅔ of the infants with congenital rubella will be free of any abnormality at birth."[19] Abnormalities that may be present include anemia and jaundice, as well as more life-threatening possibilities. The point is this: when is a possibility of deformity enough to "excuse" taking the fetus' life?

Here is a related question that should be asked: "Is being born with mental deformities worse or better than being born with a physical deformity, like missing fingers?" Because mental ability can seldom be predicted with much accuracy, even when amniocentesis proves that there is a clear genetic abnormality such as Down's syndrome, should mental-ability predictions ever be used to deny an unborn child his or her right to life?

Suppose it is 100 percent sure that a fetus has no arms, but is mentally sound—should his or her mother be allowed to abort? What if only one arm is missing, or part of one arm, or just some fingers? Where would we draw the line?

A special aspect of this exception, and perhaps the most difficult one for the pro-life side to counter, is when the child is known to be anencephalic. Because in these situations a complete brain will not be present, the child will be stillborn or will die within a matter of days no matter how much care he or she is given.[20] Anencephaly may be documented before birth, and it presents the mother with two difficult options: (1) to abort the unborn child right away or (2) to carry the child to term knowing that he or she will not have a chance of living for more than a very short time.

This author admits to some ambivalent feelings on this difficult case, just as he did in the case of pregnancies from rape. In my opinion, imminent death should not be used to justify hastening that death, most especially for someone other than yourself, although the use of life-support technologies in such cases could be seen to be "extraordinary" care that would not be demanded ethically.

Whether the unborn child was the result of a rape, or is afflicted with deformities that will mean a quick death after birth, human life should be respected. Killing an innocent human being is unethical, although it would seem cruel to condemn harshly a woman who considered an abortion in such a desperate case.

Pro-choice argument 8
Abortion should be permitted in cases where the mother finds it pleasurable to choose the sex of her child, or when fetal tissues or organs are needed to reduce the suffering of people with diseases.

Pro-life response
This pro-choice argument is really two separate arguments that have been joined together here because they both are what might be called an extreme pro-choice view—just as a pro-life denial (like this author's) of an exception for rape victims might represent an extreme pro-life viewpoint.

Abortion of a fetus of the "wrong" sex (usually female) is legally possible in the United States. Some amniocentesis centers routinely refuse to tell the mother what the child's sex is to prevent the likelihood that such a decision will be made. Others cater to women seeking just such information to abort a child of the unwanted sex.[21]

Some scientists have recently been advocating the use of aborted fetuses as sources for needed human tissues and organs. As this book is being written (1991), the U.S. government has a ban on the use of fetal tissues and organs in federally sponsored research. Some efforts have been made to get this policy reversed, with scientists claiming that fetal tissue and organs have had and will continue to have a crucial role in medical advances.[22]

One possible use for fetal tissues is represented by fetal pancreas cells, which may be used as a "cure" for diabetes in the future. Another celebrated role for fetal tissues is postulated from early research on Parkinson's disease.[23] This latter disease afflicts the nervous systems of primarily elderly people and may be mitigated by injecting brain cells from eight-week-old fetuses into the brains of patients. What if a woman were to get pregnant to get an abortion and use the brain of the fetus for treatment of a relative suffering from Parkinson's disease? Would this be ethically acceptable? Certainly under the Supreme Court's *Roe v. Wade* decision this would not be contrary to the Constitution, for no reason is required for a woman before she has an abortion at the eight-week stage of her pregnancy.

Although there is some controversy as to whether fetal tissues are that crucial to current researchers[24], this author believes that the potential uses of fetal tissues are large. Many research programs currently using animal "models" of human beings could advance if human tissues and organs were more readily available. This is one reason why pressures have been brought to bear on the federal government by certain members of Congress (chiefly Rep. Henry Waxman, California Democrat) to reverse the administration's policy against the funding of fetal tissue research. (One might ask why aborted human fetuses are so human that scientists are anxious to get their hands on them, but not human enough to be allowed the most basic human rights.)

To use fetuses as tissue and organ "farms" is to use these human beings like commodities or a mere means to help someone else reach his or her goals. That persons should not be so used is a basic argument of Kantian ethics[25] and, it might be claimed, a trait of Western civilization. Nevertheless, there is a kind of ethical consistency in the argument that because abortion is permitted for any reason during the first trimester, why should a woman not be permitted to get pregnant for the purpose of aborting the fetus? What argument can be used to prohibit such an abortion, but still permit reproductive freedom for women? For the pro-lifer the opposition to these pro-choice arguments is easier than the opposition to rape and "life-of-the-mother" exceptions. And even for pro-choice advocates these types of pro-choice arguments pose special problems; pro-choice advocates find themselves on the short side of opinion polls when these types of questions are asked.

Conclusion

I have sought to present logically pure counter-arguments against pro-choice positions, even when such counter-arguments fly in the face of public opinion polls and run counter to this author's own emotional prejudices. Pro-choice advocates also have difficulties achieving ethical purity, and the arguments being encountered here are good examples. Some pro-choice people have taken consistent positions where they reluctantly argue against their gut feelings, claiming the pro-choice position requires a woman to be allowed to abort for the most frivolous of reasons. Others compromise on ethical purity, adopting positions that are inconsistent in philosophy but are in accord with public opinion. Unfortunately, when taken as a whole, public opinion on abortion is so ethically muddled that trying to accommodate it is a detriment to those who are trying to find an ethical rationale consistent with public opinion. The tack taken by this author is to argue that innocent human life ought not be killed, except perhaps in the case of self-defense, and that abortions, even those that present heart-wrenching emotional dilemmas, cannot in the final analysis be ethically justified, even if legally tolerated.

In this chapter I have defined some key ethical terms and looked at the teleological arguments often found on the pro-choice side. Most of the pro-choice teleological arguments have been seen to be groundless, or at best flawed (e.g., when proponents of the pro-choice position look at only the short-term welfare savings and ignore the dramatic long-term economic threats inherent in their position).

Also in this chapter, the pro-life deontological position (the right-to-life argument) has been applied to counter the pro-choice teleological arguments; in every case the pro-life position has been found to be ethically superior. This type of ethical debate, however, places the pro-choice side at somewhat of a disadvantage for, as has already been discussed, deontological arguments tend to win over teleological ones in public policy battles.

By using the right-to-life deontological position against the pro-choice teleological position, the pro-choice side has in effect throughout this chapter been forced to fight with one hand tied behind its back. In the next chapter, the strong pro-choice deontological argument (the right to autonomy) will be allowed to attack the right-to-life argument completely unfettered, to see if the pro-life position can maintain its ethical supremacy in a fair fight.

Chapter 3

Right to Life versus Autonomy

In the last chapter various teleological arguments for abortion were discussed. In this chapter we will discuss the concept of autonomy, which was only cursorily addressed. It is this argument—that one has the personal liberty to make one's own decisions—that represents the root deontological argument of the pro-choice position. It is the strongest of all pro-choice ethical arguments; hence the decision by pro-choice advocates to name themselves after this pro-choice, pro-autonomy concept. It is here that the pro-life teleological and deontological arguments find their greatest ethical challenge.

Pro-choice advocates tend to see abortion as a matter of personal freedom. To limit their right to have their unborn children killed before birth is to them to limit the right to control their own bodies, which contain the unborn children. To deny women abortions, it is argued, is to deny them a choice. They wish to have the right to choose an abortion, and pro-lifers say this is a right that they should not have. Who do the pro-lifers think they are to deny women their wishes? Who does anyone think he is to tell another person a choice cannot be made?

At this point one often encounters the pro-choice argument that "you cannot legislate morality." The pro-choice advocates feel that if the pro-lifers think abortion is a choice they cannot morally make, that is their business. The pro-choicers do not want to remove the right of the pro-lifers to choose not to abort, but they want the pro-lifers to give them the freedom of choice *to* abort. The argument is that the pro-lifers are trying to force their morality on others.

First, it would be helpful to look at laws and see if we can find some that have a moral component to them. Or are laws pretty much amoral statements aimed at ordering human societies? With a quick question, we can see that all laws, especially all criminal statutes, have a moral component as a prerequisite. There are no exceptions that the pro-choice advocates can designate. The question that makes this clear is to ask people to name an action that (1) they personally feel should be a serious crime under the law *and* that (2) they do not feel is immoral. It becomes abundantly clear not only that morality is legislated, but also that there are few, if any, laws created that are not based on some moral value statement.

What pro-choicers may mean when they say you cannot legislate morality is more correctly interpreted as follows: victimless crimes are super-moralistic and should not be legislated to be crimes because no second party is harmed. A legislative initiative often mentioned by the pro-choicers is prohibition, when the manufacture, transportation, and sale of alcoholic beverages was forbidden in an effort to eliminate the victimless crime of drinking alcohol. Other so-called victimless crimes might include prostitution, sodomy, smoking marijuana, and suicide. The argument is that as long as the choices someone makes do not affect adversely another person, then even if the choices seem immoral to other people in society they should be tolerated under the law. If I want to be a prostitute, and if I am not spreading disease, why should not I have that right? If I wish to drink alcoholic beverages in my own home and am not risking anyone else's health (e.g., I am not trying to drive while intoxicated—an act that even the anti-victimless-crimes people would feel should be illegal), why should the "prohibition mentality" of others try to limit my choices?

This argument admits that some victimless crimes, like prostitution, are acceptable to society, if not to pro-choicers. Nevertheless, it may be that even pro-choicers would agree that passing laws to prohibit some victimless crimes is appropriate. For example, it might be particularly appropriate to have laws that prevent someone from eliminating his or her ability to make future choices by committing suicide. Such a law would make it easier to institutionalize people who attempt suicide but fail. Another such law might prevent someone from selling himself or herself into slavery. Here the effort to sustain the autonomy of the individual restricts the individual's right to autonomy. Society might wish to prohibit such victimless crimes insofar as they in effect reduce personal liberties within society.

Personal autonomy is indeed one of the most cherished of the freedoms that persons enjoy, but it is an overstatement to say that even that freedom should be unbridled by society. In fact there are many choices denied to persons by government—such as the freedom to shoot your neighbor or to drive your car the wrong way on a one-way street. Also, in even a cursory look at the main two competing deontological principles in the abortion debate—the right to choose versus the right to life—it is clear which of the two carries the greater moral weight.

The right to life has been called by many people the right to have rights. The living person who has no right to choose is in a poor position, but not in as poor a position as the person who is dead. The dead have lost all their choices. To allow someone the right to freedom of speech or the right to a fair trial, but not to allow him or her the right to live, is to make all the other allowed rights a mockery.

Autonomy is certainly a very important and basic right, and "liberty" is specifically mentioned in the American Declaration of Independence and in the Fourteenth Amendment to the United States Constitution, but in both documents the right to life is listed before the right to liberty: ". . . right to life, liberty, and the pursuit of happiness" (Declaration of Independence); and ". . . life, liberty, or property" (Fourteenth Amendment).

By gaining the legal permission to choose abortion, the pro-choicers do increase by one the list of liberties that they enjoy. In their personal frame of reference it technically is a "pro-choice" decision. But in the case of their sons and daughters who are destroyed by the abortionists, every one of those unborn children's future choices is destroyed with them. The net result of the pro-choice position is, therefore, a net loss of autonomous action, not an increase. As the prerogative to choose death is embraced as a right, choice is lost, just as it is in the case of allowing people to sell themselves into slavery. If the pro-choice label is appropriate for those who fight for abortion rights, then the pro-choice label is equally appropriate for those who would argue for the removal of any or all laws, even laws against slavery or stealing. After all, if the laws against stealing were removed, the list of legal choices available would increase; therefore, those who argue that stealing should be legal are "pro-choice."

This author has reached the conclusion that those who argue that they should have the right to kill another person should probably be embarrassed to use the label of "pro-choice." Liberty is important, but when used to deny life to the innocent, it borders on being reprehensible.

Just as the deontological principle of not harming the lives of others holds ethical sway over such pro-choice teleological arguments as the economic arguments listed in the previous chapter, it holds sway over the prime pro-choice deontological argument in favor of the right to autonomy. The right to life is so basic that it not only takes precedence over results-oriented pro-choice arguments, it also takes precedence over all other rights-based arguments, even the argument for autonomy.

So, is the abortion debate over? No. Perhaps the most difficult and philosophically complex aspect of the pro-choice argument is yet to be addressed.

Chapter 4

Science and Personhood

A s discussed in the previous chapter, much of the controversy about abortion revolves around the concept of
personhood. When pro-abortion-rights advocates argue that women have
a right to make their own private decisions, they are not arguing that this
right has more moral weight than the right of a person to his or her life.
Instead, they are arguing that unborn children are not truly persons and
therefore cannot have a right to life that would balance, indeed, override,
the woman's autonomous right to an abortion.

Similar assumptions regarding the nature of personhood are often
made when pro-choice advocates argue about the need to reduce unwanted children and excess population. These arguments hinge on the
assumption that the human being that is killed by the abortionist is not a
person with a right to be treated as an equal with other persons.

Personhood is a concept sometimes referred to by such terms such as
humanhood or *soul*. Each of these terms represents an attempt to define
the relationship between the biological and abstract aspects of humanity.
The centrality of the issue of personhood, as far as the abortion debate is
concerned, has been previously reported by numerous authors. William
May states that "the central issue in the abortion debate, as Paul Ramsey
forcefully notes, is not when does human life begin, but 'When does
equally protectable life begin?' "[1]

Clifford Bajema has stated the problem in the following manner: "Even
the most avid pro-abortionists agree that *life* (indeed, human life) begins
at conception. The point of disagreement has centered around the question of *when full status of humanity of personhood* begins."[2]

31

The Search for a Definition of Personhood

There have been many attempts to define the concept of personhood in hope that the definition will lend itself to a solution of the abortion debate. If the definition permits the development of criteria with which a disinterested observer is able to rule on the personhood of various human beings, then the moral obligations due to these human beings could be accurately assessed, or at least more accurately assessed than currently is possible. Some of the most common definitions of personhood found in the literature are briefly described below, followed by a general discussion that reaches a specific conclusion as to which definition is most objectively defensible.

It should be evident, however, that even when a decision is made concerning the question of personhood, the abortion debate is not necessarily ended. Proponents of similar positions on the nature of personhood may still reach contradictory positions on such questions as the proper role of government in protecting the lives of persons and so-called "potential" persons.

Postbirth Personhood

This definition of personhood not only excludes all unborn human beings, it also excludes some human beings who have been born. Joseph Fletcher assumes this position when he claims that a human being is not a person if it lacks freedom, rationality, self-determination, the ability to choose either means or ends, and a knowledge of its circumstances.[3] Michael Tooley also takes a postnatal view of personhood when he maintains that "an organism possesses a serious right to life only if it possesses the concept of a self as a continuing subject of experiences and other mental states, and believes that it is itself such a continuing entity."[4] However, Tooley has since qualified this position very slightly by stating that " . . . in view of a number of quite significant developments clustering together at around ten to twelve weeks, it may be that humans become quasi-persons at about that time."[5]

Daniel Callahan criticizes the normative basis of Fletcher's approach to ethics in general (as expressed in Fletcher's writings on "situational ethics") because Fletcher "insists that an intuitive appraisal be made in each situation."[6] Callahan also characterizes Fletcher's value-setting methodology as being determined by "unexamined predilection."[7]

Baruch Brody criticizes Tooley's definition, which Tooley himself modifies for certain human beings in special circumstances (e.g., the mentally disturbed). Brody believes that the admission of the need for modifications leaves Tooley "open to the challenge that he has arbitrarily excluded the newborn and the fetus from the class of persons."[8]

Richard Werner criticizes Tooley's position because it fails to condemn as an infringement on the rights of future generations any human action that might permit pollution to reach a point that all babies are stillborn, thus ending the human race; but it would consider an infringement of rights to have taken place if the pollution caused slightly uncomfortable living conditions. Werner appeals to intuition by pointing out that people find such a conclusion "morally more repugnant."[9]

James Hanick similarly points out that there seems to be a peculiar inconsistency in Tooley's willingness to "recognize the potential desires of persons existing in the future while ignoring the potential desires of those who, but for one's killing them, would exist in the future."[10]

Personhood at Birth

Although few contemporary philosophers have adopted this definition, it is nevertheless a very important one for it is the position taken in 1973 by the Supreme Court of the United States when ruling on a Texas anti-abortion law. In the famous *Roe v. Wade* case, the Court did not require the states to apply the concept of a right to life, as guaranteed only to *persons* under the Fourteenth Amendment, to human beings at any time before birth. The majority of the justices made this statement:

> Texas urges that, apart from the Fourteenth Amendment, life begins at conception and is present throughout pregnancy, and that, therefore, the State has a compelling interest in protecting that life from and after conception. We need not resolve the difficult question of when life begins. When those trained in the respective disciplines of medicine, philosophy, and theology are unable to arrive at any consensus, the judiciary, at this point in the development of man's knowledge, is not in a position to speculate as to the answer.[11]

The aspect of this statement that affects the question of whether life begins at conception (as defined to be synonymous with fertilization) is discussed later under the fertilization definition of personhood.

After saying it could not answer the question of when life begins, the Supreme Court referred to historical confusions, contradictory theological

theories, and past legal statements about the point in the development of
the fetus where human rights could be found to have been granted. The
Court thus moved from a medical approach to the question of life and fell
back on a legal and historical approach, first concluding that the fetus had
no human rights under the Constitution: ". . . the word *person,* as used in
the Fourteenth Amendment, does not include the unborn."[12] The Court
also concluded that ". . . the unborn have never been recognized in the
law as persons in the whole sense. In view of all this, we do not agree
that, by adopting one theory of life, Texas may override the rights of the
pregnant woman that are at stake."[13]

It is not the purpose of this chapter to review historical arguments for
or against abortion, although there is ample evidence that the Supreme
Court did fail to consider many historical facts that would have altered its
conclusions.[14] Instead, this chapter asks normative questions: Should
abortion be illegal from now on? Should the biological human being in
the womb be granted human rights, including the right to life, equal with
those who have (just) passed out of the womb?

The result of the Court's decision in *Roe v. Wade* is that the citizens of
the United States are not constitutionally restricted from procuring full-
term abortions. The Supreme Court did not permit states the option of
proscribing abortions before viability, or even after viability if the mother's
health was threatened even in a minor way. If the states elected to pass no
laws to address the later stages of pregnancy, then the pregnant woman,
in consultation with her physician, would have the right to an abortion
one second before birth. One second after birth, and the child would have
a constitutional right to life equal to the woman's right.

It might appear at first that the Supreme Court took a viability definition
of personhood (the next definition to be discussed), although a closer
reading of the decision yields ample evidence that it is the state and not
the fetus that has rights between viability and birth and that the exercise
of these limited state rights is not based on any constitutional guarantee
of a right to life before birth.

Many investigators, including Wertheimer[15] and Willke and Willke[16],
have rejected this definition on the grounds that it is only descriptive of
the human being's environment (in the womb or out of the womb) and
not of any personhood-related attributes of human beings.

Viability Personhood

This definition maintains that personhood begins at a point when the
developing human being is capable of living independently from his or

her mother. Brody, who does not himself support this position, has stated the reasoning behind this definition in the following way:

> How can anything be a human being if it is incapable of an independent existence? Only when the fetus becomes viable apart from its mother is it a human being.[17]

Kristin Luker, in her extensive study of the pro-choice and pro-life viewpoints, underscores the importance of viability to the pro-choice movement's philosophy:

> For most pro-choice people, the personhood of the embryo does not exist at conception, but it does develop at some later time. The pro-choice view of personhood is thus a *gradualist* one. An embryo may not be a full person until it is viable (capable of sustaining its own life if born prematurely), but it has the rights of a potential person at all times, and those rights increase in moral weight as the pregnancy continues. (Wearing an IUD is morally acceptable to pro-choice people because they consider very early embryos to be little more than fertilized eggs.)[18]

This concept of a "potential" person will be encountered again under the subheading of brain function personhood and will be a major topic of a later discussion.

Wertheimer[19] has pointed out a basic problem with this definition by noting that it will vary in its application as medical technology develops better techniques for sustaining the fetus. The viability definition is a measure of the medical art, and not of the inherent qualities of the fetus. This definition therefore has flaws similar to those claimed to be present in the "personhood at birth" position, in that both are relying on extra-organism factors.

K. D. Whitehead has posed a different aspect of this same counter-argument: He claims that the acceptance of the viability criterion would require society to deny personhood to adults who "temporarily require an oxygen tent or an iron lung in order to survive."[20] Test-tube babies born as a result of *in vitro* fertilization also pose problems for this definition of personhood because *in vitro* fertilization results in an individual human being who is alive apart from his or her mother.

Brain Function Personhood and Potential Persons

Proponents of the position that personhood begins when the embryonic brain first produces brain waves include Baruch Brody and, more recently,

Hans-Martin Sass. Sass argues that the beginning of life should be norma-
tively consistent with the ending of life. Because brain death is a rational
definition of when a person has died, according to Sass, it is reasonable to
assert that a fetus becomes human when its brain begins to function. Brain
function could be the criterion for deciding when a fetus may be considered a live human being and, thus, the criterion for settling the abortion
argument.[21]

Brody, whose writings predate those of Sass, also maintains that a fetus
does not become a person until its brain begins to function, usually as
evidenced by the presence of brain waves that are detectable by an
electroencephalograph machine (i.e., at about six-weeks gestation). He
defends his position by first posing the question "What properties are
such that their loss would mean the going out of existence or death of a
person?"[22] Based on his answer to this question (a person is dead only "if
there has been an irreparable cessation of spontaneous and natural cardiac
and respiratory functions and there has been an irreparable cessation of
brain function"[23]), he goes on to support a brain function definition for
the beginning of personhood because *all* of these capabilities are obviously not present in the fetus until the last one, brain function, is present.
However, Brody also allows for a definition of death developed by Paul
Ramsey; namely, that death does not take place until each of the three
aforementioned functions (heart, respiratory, and brain) has irreparably
ceased.[24] This distinction could therefore bring the time of personhood
up to when the fetus acquires the first capability, a functioning heart, or
as early as two or three weeks after fertilization.

Brody has yet another approach to using brain function as a means of
determining the point of personhood:

> One of the characteristics essential to a human being is the capacity for
> conscious experience, at least at a primitive level. Before the sixth week, as
> far as we know, the fetus does not have this capacity. Thereafter, as the
> electroencephalographic evidence indicates, it does. Consequently, that is
> the time at which the fetus becomes a human being.[25]

Andre Hellegers has characterized approaches such as Brody's as
"sloppy thinking."[26] He points out that brain function measurements taken
near the end of a person's life are used only to make prognostications as
to the likelihood that that particular human being will have the capacity to
think in the future. If there are no longer any brain waves, the diagnosis is
that the person is dead. This same diagnosis would not result from
learning that an early human embryo has no measurable brain waves, for

the embryo has an excellent likelihood of having a future capacity to think.

John Dedek[27] and Daniel Callahan[28] make similar objections, noting that it is the irreversibility of a coma and not the coma itself that brings one to conclude that death has taken place.

Brody attempts to deal with this objection by noting that "it never considers the possibility that actually engaging in some human activity, in addition to the potential (in any sense) of doing so, is required if the entity in question is to be human."[29] Continuing on this theme, he makes the following claim:

> What is essential for being human is the possession of the potential for human activities that comes with having the structures required for a functioning brain. It is this potential that the fetus acquires at (or perhaps slightly before) the time that its brain starts functioning, and it is this potential that the newly conceived fetus does not have.[30]

Brody therefore uses the concept of "future capacity" or "potential capacity" in a more restricted sense than those who seek to discredit his brain function definition of personhood. For him, and also for Wertheimer,[31] the word *human* has significance insofar as it applies to the present. Those who use the phrases *potential human* or *potential personhood* are only admitting that personhood does not currently exist. It is possible to argue that the functioning human brain is not the essential capability of the fetus that makes him or her a person, but it is not possible to select it or any other characteristic as being the essential one and then claim that because the fetus will *eventually* obtain that characteristic the fetus is a "potential person" with higher moral claims to a right to life. Either the unborn child has reached personhood, or the unborn child is not to be afforded personhood rights; and either death is the opposite of human life, rather than of potential human life, or the terms death and life must inherently contradict each other.

Blastocyst Personhood

This interesting definition of personhood postulates the granting of personhood rights shortly after fertilization, but before implantation (about one week). The embryo in this early stage is sometimes referred to by the confusing term *pre-embryo* (presumably studied by pre-embryologists?!). The justification for this delay is based on the apparent fact that the identical twinning process takes place at this time. Ramsey grants this blastocyst, or "primitive streak," modification to his idea of a genetic definition of personhood.[32] James Hanick uses this argument to dispute the genetic basis for personhood because individuality, an almost universally agreed on aspect of personhood, is not provable at fertilization.[33] Hanick admits that scientific developments might someday prove that there is individuality of both twins from conception on, but he maintains that until such proof is available the genetic arguments are unpersuasive.

Willke and Willke discount the blastocyst definition without resorting to a claim that both twins are distinctly present from fertilization: "One way of considering it is that the original human zygote . . . can be considered in effect the parent of the new human being."[34] Although such asexual reproduction does not conform to the usual view of human zoology, it is a biological mechanism very commonly encountered among animal species.

Another problem with accepting the blastocyst definition is the fact that it fails to provide a justification for excluding from protection those zygotes that will not undergo twinning, except to say that they are indistinguishable from the other zygotes until the blastocyst stage. This is not really an ethical argument for killing the majority of human beings who are indisputably individuals from fertilization onward, for it fails to define what these human zygotes are if they are not individuals of the next generation. In other words, the fact that some cells in an embryo can be separated from the others and produce a second or third individual does not negate the human individuality of each of the identical twins or triplets or of the organism that gave rise to the twins. Twinning produces a double-worth; it does not reduce by some percentage the human worth of the embryo from which the twins came.

Conception (Fertilization) Personhood

Many religious denominations have a strong position in favor of defining fertilization as the beginning of personhood. Some of these are mentioned in the appendix to the pro-life section of this text. They tend to be based on a close interpretation of holy writings believed to be handed down by the Deity.

An interesting conception definition is that of the famous author Pearl Buck. She believed that abortion should be prohibited from fertilization on, not because of any specific definition of personhood so much as because of the danger that she believed any other practice will hold for the human race:

> I fear the power of choice over life or death at human hands. I see no human being whom I could ever trust with such power—not myself, not any other. Human wisdom, human integrity are not great enough. Since the fetus is a creature already alive and in the process of development, to kill it is to choose death over life. At what point shall we allow this choice? For me to answer is—at no point, once life has begun. At no point, I repeat, either as life begins or as life ends, for we who are human beings cannot, for our own safety, be allowed to choose death, life being all we know. Beyond life lie only faith and surmise, but not knowledge. Where there is no knowledge except for life, decision for death is not safe for the human race.[35]

Others support the conception definition of personhood because fertilization is the beginning of the individual human being's genetic existence. Paul Ramsey expresses this position, writing that "genetics teaches us that we were from the beginning what we essentially still are in every cell and in every generally human attribute and in every individual attribute."[36]

Opponents of the conception definition are of course as numerous as the proponents of other positions. Callahan offers a complex argument against the typical Christian viewpoint because he considers it to neglect the proper role of moral discourse—proper even within the Christian view of life. He criticizes those who base their moral theory of the "sanctity of life" on disclosures from God (e.g., through scripture or divine imposition of this theory on men) and labels this approach as a "falsification of consciousness."[37] He reaches this conclusion based on an assessment that even God-given rules such as "Thou shalt not kill" are permitted exceptions, proving to him that all "moral rules are human artifacts."[38]

Dedek maintains that revelation is not a matter of God imposing certain moral or doctrinal positions, but rather it is a supernatural insight into humanity's true self-understanding at its most profound level. Dedek therefore rules out Callahan's argument that moral rules are dependent on arbitrary decisions or majority votes.[39]

The above-mentioned position taken by Buck seems to be a statement of pessimism that a realistic definition of personhood will ever be found, or at least a statement that the definition would be applicable only if society were willing to take grave risks. This argument therefore will be discussed when the "nondefinition" positions are examined later.

In regard to Ramsey's genetic argument for fertilization personhood, Brody again calls upon his "present" view of potentiality to voice an objection: "Even if it is true that all of these properties are determined by chromosomal structure . . . it does not follow that the fetus already has all of these properties."[40]

Needless to say, the most important group to reject the conception definition of personhood is the United States Supreme Court, as mentioned above under the "personhood at birth" position. The Court decided that the Texas law's endorsement of a theory that life begins at conception should be discounted based on a series of historical anecdotes, much from eras before the Middle Ages, showing how various societies had been unsure of biological facts in the past. The Court, as has already been quoted, concluded that there was no way to determine at this time "the difficult question of when life begins."

Discussion of Definitions

Perhaps the most alarming definition of personhood is the postbirth definition. It is based on such subjective criteria that it seems to pose a host of social errors. The list of criteria, as has been mentioned already, might fail to grant even toddlers the right to life and would raise the question of who should get the privilege of defining the list's contents? If human rights can be given and denied based on nonscientific criteria, then anyone could be the victim of a postbirth "abortion." The label of subhuman or nonhuman has been used often throughout history to justify the denial of freedoms and, eventually, the right to life of large classes of people. For example, during the slavery years it was commonly questioned "whether the Negro was actually a human being,"[41] and "in the 1930s and early 1940s many whites still believed that blacks were an inferior people."[42] The infamous *Dred Scott* decision of the United States Supreme Court said Negroes could enjoy none of the rights of the Constitution.[43]

Similar examples of groups for which dehumanizing social definitions have been used could be listed—American Indians; retarded people; handicapped newborns; and Jews, Negroes, and Gypsies during Hitler's Third Reich. During Hitler's reign, some people were so robbed of their human rights that they became legal subjects for medical experiments, as if they were so much laboratory tissue.[44] This is perhaps the ultimate stage of the state's applying its criteria for personhood to a group—to have members of that group involuntarily used for experiments even while they are on their way to be robbed and executed.

Be eschewing any definition of personhood that cannot be scientifically applied, a Pandora's box is opened, and each of us had better lobby for a spot on the commission that defines the criteria for personhood if we want to be sure of our human rights.

The next topic to discuss is the concept of "potential" persons, which represents a complicating aspect in the search for a definition of personhood. This complication was evident above in the brain function definition postulated by Brody.

Brody's oversight is not in his insistence on a present-tense definition of personhood potential but in the inconsistency between this insistence and his definition for brain death. Because there are physical conditions that can result in temporary loss of brain function (e.g., hypothermia— low body temperature caused by exposure to cold), Brody and Ramsey were forced to add the word *irreparable* to their definition of death. Without the inclusion of this word in the definition of death, hypothermia victims would be considered dead even though they might still have a good chance of regaining all of their faculties in a short time. But the word irreparable implies the concept of future capabilities, which Brody has excluded from his definition of when personhood begins. To be consistent, he must either drop the word irreparable from his definition of death and allow the "abortion" of hypothermia victims, or he must accept a definition of life that includes future "potential" and answers the criticisms of Hellegers, Dedek, and Callahan.

If it were argued that to have personhood is to have had a functioning brain in the past and to have the potential for a functioning brain in the future, the counter-argument then becomes that this definition does not protect the hypothermia victim from being killed before brain waves reappear.[45]

Nevertheless, there are two key arguments contained in Brody's position that cannot be denied: that the definition of life must be consistent with the definition of death, and that the potential person, *if such a concept could exist,* is by definition not a real person yet. But the crucial question still remains: what is a real, nonpotential person?

Recall that in its *Roe v. Wade* decision the Supreme Court expressed grave doubts that the question of when life begins is possible to answer in a medical way. The unusual aspect about the Court's claim is that not only can medical scientists answer the question of when life begins, even a high school biology student can answer it—though it admittedly is a trick question when it is phrased in just that way. The answer to the question "When does life begin?" is *never*. Life has never been observed to "begin," it simply continues as an unbroken chain back to the dawn of creation. Life does not spring up from the nonliving world—that is, the theory of "spontaneous generation" that has been discarded by all scientists for more than a hundred years. The mineral world has never been observed to turn into the animal or vegetable world.

The Supreme Court might have been wiser to frame the question as follows: At what point did each of us begin our existence as a live organism? Or, more specifically, at what point is the chain of life that has continued unbroken from generation to generation passed on to each of us from the previous generation?

If the question is asked correctly, the answer is obvious. As any biology student knows, the only time that our parents' individual biological natures merge into a single biological nature is at the completion of the fertilization process. There is no other candidate for the point at which our individuality as biological humans begins.

If the Supreme Court had not judged Texas's stance that life begins at fertilization to be out of order, it would have had difficulty in ruling that these biological humans were devoid of human rights until they had been born. The only way that those who wished to grant abortion rights to women could philosophically defend such an unethical position would be to remove the fetus from the list of moral agents, "persons," that the law had to recognize. If the unborn children were persons, they would scuttle the effort to revise the abortion laws in all fifty states of the Union.

Recognizing the beginning of individual life to be at the completion of the fertilization process provides the strongest possible definition of personhood. It is the only definition based on a biologically provable event of substance, not just relative capability. The other definitions are based either on subjective opinions, like Fletcher's postbirth humanhood criteria and the Supreme Court's *Roe v. Wade* arguments, or on some stage of the fetus's biological development (e.g., the appearance of brain waves) for which it is difficult to see why a developing human being in his or her mother's womb one second before that stage should be considered so significantly different from a moral and legal standpoint.

Fertilization is not just another activity in the development of a fetus, it is the point where the life of the previous generation becomes the beginning of the next. Two cells from our parents—cells that were, in a way, less representative of our parents' total genetic condition than the other types of cells in their bodies—these two cells, half-genetic-complement gametes with a maximum longevity measured in days, came together and formed a genetic and protoplasmic unit that could live for a hundred years.

As Ramsey has argued, this new unit is genetically unique from his or her parents. The zygote's genetic code will determine when the blastocyst stage will be reached, when the brain waves will begin, and when viability will come about. All of the biological events will be gradual and impossible to use rationally to draw hard lines for deciding when the right to life begins. The beginning of each individual's life will be the point at which the right to life can be granted, and the point at which the mystery of life is strongest. It is the one biological, scientifically provable event in the individual's existence that is most significant and most crucial. Fertilization is not only the most significant, scientifically provable biological event in each individual life, it is also an event that will not be pushed back by technology (as the viability definition of personhood can be.[46])

It has been said that "self-reproducing, self-organizing cellular material is the common denominator of all living things."[47] The ability to reproduce is considered a key aspect of the definition of living things. Fertilization is the fulfillment of that key biological quality.

But what about the argument that was postulated in the "brain wave" definition of personhood; namely, that the definition of death should be consistent with the definition of life. This is a strong argument, and one that is so obvious that it must be accepted if the terms life and death are to mean anything.

When does death take place? It is true that many states have adopted a brain-death definition of death, but is that an accurate definition? Is it not true that a human being whose brain has been destroyed can be maintained on a respirator for long periods? Can we look at such people and say that they are not alive? The heart is beating, the flesh is warm to the touch, they can metabolize sugar put into their veins—these are clearly not attributes we assign to any portion of the mineral world.

Now it might be argued that such people have lost all opportunity to exist as a functioning biological unit, especially when all the unifying physiological systems of the body, such as the neurological, circulatory, and respiratory systems, have ceased to maintain homeostasis.[48] But even as the body is placed in the coffin and lowered into the ground, the body still has cells that function somewhat independently from these unifying biological systems. For instance, hair continues to grow.

A body that is still growing hair is not dead in a purely biological sense, although those cells still functioning will soon cease functioning. Another way to look at this from a purely biological stance is that as long as any cell is still able to carry out its genetically programmed function, the body is obviously not yet completely dead.

The point is not that society should delay burying anyone until every cell in his or her body has died. There is certainly some logic in abandoning care for the cells once all chance for homeostasis is lost. The point is that death does not take place on a cellular level until the genetic program is disrupted. Brain waves are a convenient method for making a determination of death, thanks to the fact that heart and lung machines can prolong some complex unifying systems even without a functioning brain. Brody and Sass are right to argue that the legal and moral definition of death should logically parallel the definition of life, but they err by pointing to the socially popular definition rather than to a scientific one. When the scientific definition is used, it complements the logic of recognizing fertilization as the beginning of life.

A final argument for the fertilization definition of personhood is that it completely settles the argument concerning "potential" persons. In effect, one of the best arguments for the fertilization definition is the fact that it makes moot the potentiality concept with which the Supreme Court and others have struggled so valiantly. It simply is not possible to talk of the "potential" person as long as the point of personhood is recognized to be at the beginning of the biological existence of the human individual. In such a case there is no time before the beginning of personhood for the morally confusing concept of "potential" personhood to play havoc with the ethical and public policy decision-making process.

Anti-Definition Positions

Looking back over the various definitions of personhood, it is clear that the formulation of a definition is not easy. Certain of the arguments were shown to be false because they were based on a scientific half-truth. Unfortunately, these refutations could be deflated by simply adding an exception to the general rule. For example, Brody could answer the hypothermia counter-argument by adding the statement "except in the case of hypothermia" to his definitions, an approach Ramsey seems to have taken to deal with the problem of the blastocyst. Brody could also simply ignore any intuitive repulsion generated by the idea of "aborting" the hypothermia victim and thereby retain consistency and scientific accuracy.

Cannot this same ignoring of intuition produce consistent ethical positions for virtually all definitions of personhood? Are not all refutations of such positions only restatements of our intuitively derived, but possibly still very consistent, definitions of personhood? Can even the strong arguments for the fertilization definition be challenged based on epistemological grounds—grounds that will argue that even the best definition of personhood cannot be truly *known* to be true?

There are those who maintain that indeed there is no nonarbitrary definition of personhood. If they are correct, then arguments for or against abortion may only be convincing when (1) the debaters share a common definition of when a human being becomes a person, allowing teleological and deontological arguments to carry the decision against abortion, or (2) the debate is based on an argument that applies to no particular definition of personhood, without necessarily ignoring the importance of the personhood concept.

In their searches for a definition of personhood, both Hanick and Dedek eventually came to support an anti-definition position; that is, they came to believe that a definition could not be derived. Hanick concluded that "unless they [the philosophers] somehow first change our moral practices, which in part shape our existing concept of person, their proposals are at best of only academic interest.[49]

Dedek writes:

> There is no way that one can be certain from the evidence available. This, I think, is the only honest conclusion one can draw from the empirical and philosophical data. What one does with this conclusion on the practical ethical level is another matter.[50]

Wertheimer also reaches this conclusion, but takes a path that is particularly comprehensive. He begins by looking at what he labels the "conservative" position (a pro-life position) that the fetus is a full-fledged person from conception, and he points out that only such a lofty definition of a fetus could possibly justify the prohibition of abortion. In his opinion, abortion has "staggering social costs."[51]

Wertheimer next examines and discards various arguments that he calls "liberal" (pro-choice positions). To the argument that restrictive abortion laws cause untold grief in society, Wertheimer takes the deontological view that simply the amount of grief produced by an action cannot be considered sufficient justification for acting unjustly. Otherwise, he argues, the same argument could be used to permit the elimination of grief-causing parent-persons as well as grief-causing fetus-persons. This kind of utilitarian argument against restrictive abortion laws is acceptable to Wertheimer only if the fetus is not a person. As a nonutilitarian, he refuses to justify the means by calculating the benefits of the ends.

Wertheimer, who eventually reaches a pro-choice conclusion, refutes other liberal pro-choice arguments. He throws out the accusation that conservatives are heartless by noting that it is inappropriate to call someone heartless who is only trying to protect innocent persons from being killed. He discards the liberal argument that conservatives should believe what they want, pointing out that to the conservative the issue is not one of personal freedom of belief or of "victimless" crimes, but one of civil rights. The conservative seeks to protect the right to life of an innocent person who is considered by the conservative to be a full-fledged victim.

Wertheimer concludes that, given the conservative premise that the fetus is a person, the conservative position on abortion adheres to the dictates of common sense. The liberals' exasperation with this position is based on the liberals' inability to see that premise as anything but nonsense. The conservative, of course, takes an equally dim view of the liberal premise that declines to equate humanity with personhood until human beings reach viability or are born. In Wertheimer's words:

> Both liberals and conservatives think it is wrong to kill an innocent person except when other human lives would be lost. So neither party will reform their speech habits regarding the fetus unless that moral principle is re-worded in a way that vouchsafes their position on abortion. Any stipulated definition can be recommended only by appealing to the very matters under dispute. . . . The correctness of any such definition must first be tested against our judgments of particular cases, and on some of those judgments people disagree; so the argument using such a definition which tries to settle that disagreement can only beg the question.[52]

Wertheimer thus makes a comprehensive argument explaining why he feels the many different definitions of personhood that have been dis-cussed previously fail to end the debate. His position is that when these definitions are examined closely, they all, whether liberal, conservative, or moderate, argue that abortions can justly be prohibited after point X in the human development process, not because a human with X is valuable in an objective sense, but because humans with X just seem to be persons. All of these arguments, insofar as they are internally consistent and not based on scientific falsehood, seem equally weak and equally strong. Wertheimer therefore concludes that people find some of these arguments unequally logical only because of the various ways people subjectively respond to the same facts.

Wertheimer predicts that, because of the minimal range of *interactions* possible between adults and unborn human beings, it is unlikely that there will ever be a convincing justification of either the liberal or conservative positions on personhood. He defends this claim by examin-ing the case of racism and concluding that racism is not logically and morally defensible, even though there are definite similarities between the arguments against racism (a race definition of personhood rights) and the arguments against abortion. His point is that everyone can be justifiably expected to reach the same conclusion on racism; namely, that other races possess full-fledged personhood because of the indisputable experience that is available in the form of interaction with human beings of those races. However, because the fetus is out of sight, interaction is not possible to the same extent, and the liberal and conservative arguments therefore debate under a handicap. (In this side argument, the pro-choice Wertheimer seems to switch inexplicably to a priority for subjective experience over objective logic, thus avoiding any linkage between abortion and racism.)

Wertheimer ends his treatise, almost as an aside, with an argument that restrictive abortion laws are illegitimate. Noting that it would not be rational for citizens to allow the state to have coercive powers that were not rationally justified, he puts the burden of proof on the state to justify that the fetus is a person in light of the fact that "without question, the present abortion laws seriously restrict the freedom and diminish the welfare of the citizenry."[53]

Discussion of Wertheimer's and Buck's Positions

Even though Wertheimer says that his conclusion applies only to the state and does not cast any reproach on individuals who advocate abortion restrictions, it seems that he himself has begged the question by basing his argument on the premise that abortion laws diminish the welfare of citizens. The question now becomes "Who is a citizen to Wertheimer?"

Does Wertheimer really maintain that the utility of an action should be calculated only insofar as that action affects persons who are also citizens? If this is what he means, then he must also maintain that laws prohibiting U.S. citizens from robbing visiting Canadian millionaires are also untenable. If, as appears much more likely, Wertheimer means "person" where he says "citizen," then he can no longer make the claim that abortion laws clearly diminish the welfare of citizens (read "persons").

This argument and counter-argument illustrates clearly the aspect of the abortion debate that makes the debate doubly difficult to resolve; namely, the fact that the absence of a definition of personhood equally undermines the philosophical foundations of teleology and deontology. This point has been discussed in previous chapters. Wertheimer, however, seems to overlook this point when, speaking as a deontologist, he refutes the liberal utilitarian's argument of "untold grief to society" by saying that the level of grief is irrelevant when justice to persons is at stake. He could have made a more persuasive argument against this utilitarian position by noting that without an accurate definition of *who* is in society, the utilitarians themselves really do not know how to calculate griefs or benefits.

As has been discussed, conservative definition (pro-life) utilitarians and liberal definition (pro-choice) utilitarians will reach entirely different estimates of total grief when looking at the abortion issue, so Wertheimer's appeal to a deontological argument, which the utilitarians will consider irrelevant, is not necessary.

This illustrates a possible flaw in the utilitarian position taken by Buck. She basically concludes that abortion should be illegal because if it were not it would threaten to cause excessive grief. Although it is not clear from her few short statements on the topic of abortion whether this grief would be caused by killing innocent fetuses with personhood or because killing fetuses lacking personhood might jeopardize the rights of future persons, it seems likely it was the latter. If it were the former, her position is flawed because it is only another case of the utilitarians' dilemma of how to calculate grief. If her position is the latter, she is in effect making an interesting claim that even utilitarians with a liberal definition of personhood should conclude that levels of actual, present grief caused by restricting abortions are preferable to the average forecasted levels of grief once the door is opened to killing fetuses who are considered to be persons by large segments of the society.

This interpretation of Buck's position seems to be the only argument encountered in the above summary of the debate over defining personhood (other than Wertheimer's pro-choice position) that attempts to achieve any kind of persuasiveness apart from arguments that attempt to set a point when the fetus develops into a person. However, it might appear to apply only to utilitarians and not to deontologists who restrict the application of calculations of benefits and grief when basic rights are at stake. Also, Buck's position might hinge on an assumption that could be difficult to prove; namely, that society could not keep the practice of killing fetuses judged not to be persons from degrading into a situation where people who undisputedly have personhood are left out of utilitarian calculations and are killed.

Another closely related assumption that could support Buck's fears is the notion that society would undergo a creeping transformation to a point where humans with undisputed personhood were never killed, but where the definition of personhood was construed to benefit an elite segment of society.

Support for such a "slippery slope" claim would have to be based on evidence of a sharp correlation between the initiation of similar stimuli and the production of the feared results in other societies, or on a clearly strong logical correlation between the arguments used to justify the desired social policy and the undesired one. Buck does not provide any specifics along these lines.

To see if there might be a deontological argument that can claim inter-definition persuasiveness, a return to Wertheimer's pro-abortion argument is in order. In that argument, which suffered from being founded on a utilitarian premise that failed to distinguish between citizens and persons, Wertheimer brought up the concept of "burden of proof." It might seem unfair for him to use the concept to support one side, however, when each side is pleading for a course of action perceived by the other side to be a violation of basic rights or of utilitarian logic.

Both sides in such a dispute feel with equal justification that the burden of proof lies on the other side, that is, the side that wants to ignore the true rights of (perceived) persons.

The two keys to Wertheimer's argument are (1) the high social costs of abortion laws, a point that was shown to be unprovable given the lack of definition of personhood, and (2) the position that the state should not pass an abortion law restricting personal freedom when high costs result, unless the immoral nature of abortion can be proved. It seems likely that Wertheimer would agree with the position that even when true social costs are unknown, the state still should not restrict personal freedom—unless the preservation of justice is *proven* to be at stake by not restricting it. This is a deontological alteration of his argument, using justice rather than high social costs, and at face value it seems to be a strong argument.

Looked at from another perspective, once the utilitarian concerns have been neutralized by the realization that the personhood of the people whose griefs are being measured is in dispute, there are two positions for society to consider:

Position 1. To require *proof of justice* (i.e., proof that killing a fetus is just) before permitting abortion, or

Position 2. To require *proof of injustice* (i.e., proof that killing a fetus is unjust) before prohibiting abortion.

Both of these approaches to the rational role for society are severely hampered by their inability to provide proofs of justice or injustice without any objective definition of personhood. Nevertheless, depending on which approach is chosen, the concept of a "burden of proof" will fall to one or the other side in the abortion debate.

Wertheimer might argue that the second position is superior in that it will not result in any further state restrictions on liberty, that is, on the right to autonomy. However, the pro-life side can argue that the second position permits restrictions on a right greater than autonomy in that it permits individuals to deprive other individuals of the right to life. Unjust restrictions on personal rights can be a result of too much liberty being granted to antagonists as much as a result of too much state intervention in rightful autonomy. In the absence of a nonarbitrary definition of personhood, the stronger of these two deontological positions must be the one that offers less risk of injustice.

It therefore seems likely that the deontologist will conclude that in the case of abortion proof of justice (position 1) is required because restrictive abortion laws are aimed at protecting a "higher order" right (the right to life) and (2) the arguments for no laws are based on an effort to protect a "lower-order" right (autonomy). The pro-life position on abortion surpasses the pro-choice position because the conservative position promises a greater possibility of maximizing justice in society. If society were to choose a route that has a lesser chance than another route of maximizing justice, society would belittle the deontological concept of justice and human rights.

This argument is not based on the condition that a majority of Americans must agree to the pro-life view that personhood begins at fertilization. The burden of proof argument presented above is based on appeals to the concept of human rights and other deontological principles, not on any system of government. As long as the preservation of life is agreed to have an intrinsically higher value than the preservation of the right to personal autonomy, an irreversible hierarchy given that life is a prerequisite for autonomy, then the logical deontological, human rights position must be the pro-life position. Even a 100 percent vote for a pro-choice policy cannot overcome the ethical, deontological consequences that an objective definition of personhood is not available (other than biological humanness), any more than such a vote could make racism or anarchy into a truly just national policy.

A related but slightly weaker argument that is sometimes made for the fertilization definition of personhood is that for some proponents it is not really an effort to define personhood at all. The argument here is that *because* attempts to delineate when a human being is not a person will always result in nonscientific, arbitrary conclusions, all individual human beings, no matter what their age, sex, race, and so forth, should by default be considered persons until proven otherwise. Here the concept of a burden of proof is applied in a second and more obvious way than in its above-mentioned use for determining which position must justify restrictions on basic rights and liberties.

In the first application of the burden-of-proof argument it was assumed that both pro-life and pro-choice proponents had admitted the equal logic behind each other's (arbitrary) definitions of personhood. In this application, the pro-life proponent argues that he or she has *no* definition of personhood and that, because to a certain extent any definition will be arbitrary, all human beings must be granted the right to life—at least until the liberal can scientifically or logically prove that any given individual human being indeed does not exist as an entity which deserves the name *person*.

This final position claims the pro-choice and the pro-life sides have gone beyond the proper boundaries of discourse by trying to adopt a specific definition. But whereas conservatives who argue that personhood exists from conception can make specific deontological *and* teleological/ utilitarian decisions based on that definition, proponents of this last position cannot reach pro-life utilitarian conclusions so easily. They are vulnerable to pro-choice claims that in the absence of a scientifically provable definition of personhood, utilitarian calculations of benefits must conclude that restrictive abortion laws cause grief to a significant segment of society (in particular, pregnant females), whereas abortion only *might* produce greater grief by threatening a group of "possible" humans. In other words, if instead of saying that fertilization is the beginning of personhood a pro-life advocate says that no definition of personhood is supportable, and assuming the pro-life advocate does not want to dispute the obvious claim that pregnant females have personhood rights, then the pro-life advocate no longer has unborn-persons to balance against the pregnant-female-persons in utilitarian calculations, unless the claim is stated as follows:

> Women have personhood and the right to life and to autonomy; the unborn *may* have a right to life. Because the right to life is so much more important than the right to autonomy, and because there is a possibility that the unborn has a right to life, the unborn should not be aborted.

Pro-choice deontologists may also attempt to build on this utilitarian calculus when faced with this last, weaker, pro-life position, but they will still find themselves reversed by the maximization of justice (justice being a deontological concept) argument already discussed.

Conclusions and Comments

The crux of the abortion controversy is the necessity of establishing a definition of personhood as the base of virtually all ethical obligations and the fact that all criminal law is based at least in part on a moral assessment of these obligations. The abortion debate largely centers around the need for a definition of personhood that is not arbitrary, but due to the very nature of personhood such a definition is apparently beyond the reach of man. To be universally convincing, therefore, arguments for or against abortion must recognize the centrality of the concept of personhood without being based on any particular definition of personhood. A few such arguments have been examined, with conclusions resulting in support for the pro-life, anti-abortion position.

It is quite possible, given the level of philosophical sophistication that such arguments require and the current level of sociopolitical upheaval over the issue of abortion, that one of the most likely opportunities for society to reach a consensus on the issue will be for society to first adopt a definition of personhood. That is probably one reason the issue stayed dormant during the first half of the century, for the fertilization definition was not being challenged by any significant segment of the population who felt their right to choice was being infringed. Unfortunately, it is probably too late to regain even this most likely opportunity for consensus in the near future, although a systematic look at the debate does lend philosophical, ethical, and scientific support for the historical position that fertilization is the beginning of personhood.

The prospect therefore appears to be that throughout the near future there will be a majority of people who believe that the government condones either the killing of innocent persons or the unjustified restriction of women's right to autonomy. The former situation historically is the most dangerous to a society, although of course neither situation is desirable.

Chapter 5

Summary of Conclusions

The pro-life position in regard to induced abortion has been endorsed on the principles that the right to life has supremacy over all other ethical arguments and that this right begins at fertilization. The specific steps of reasoning were

(Chapter 2) Teleological pro-life arguments were typically seen to have strong precedence over the teleological pro-choice arguments, and the deontological right-to-life argument was seen to be stronger than the teleological pro-choice arguments in every case.

(Chapter 3) The deontological pro-life argument was seen to be superior in ethical weight to the pro-choice deontological argument.

(Chapter 4) The argument that the unborn child did not possess personhood from fertilization onward, and thus could not really claim the right to life, was found to be false.

Many side-arguments have not been addressed, and it is doubtful that they could be addressed completely without taking several volumes. The effort has been aimed at reviewing the primary arguments and counter-arguments and analyzing them in as systematic a fashion as such a complex topic would permit.

In closing it must be admitted that even when one reaches an understanding that fertilization is the beginning of individual human life and the rights of personhood, many dilemmas remain. Among those mentioned are the emotional dilemmas that a fertilization definition of personhood presents: What may seem to be a strict approach to drawing ethical conclusions about the horrendous personal and social problems surrounding rape and pregnancies that risk the life of the mother. The most ethically pure solutions to these problems are unpopular and are not emotionally easy to champion. The fact that this is so is not really mitigated by the realization that the most consistent pro-choice ethical position faces its own public opinion dilemmas, such as when it gives a pregnant woman the right to choose abortion in the late stages of pregnancy or as a matter of convenience.

Solving these issues cannot be relegated solely to the policy analyst or philosopher, for there are ample political ramifications and public consensus-building dilemmas separate from those usually addressed in the rarefied atmosphere of the philosopher's or the policy-analyst's study. In the final analysis, the abortion problem weighs most heavily on those who are facing a crisis (as opposed to an inconvenient) pregnancy, for even those who seek an abortionist do not view the task with feelings of relish. The abortion option, despite the rhetoric and slogans often heard, is really viewed as only the best of various undesirable alternatives.

Whether or not the destruction of an unborn child is permitted as one of the options given to a pregnant woman, everyone individually and collectively should make sure that the pregnant woman has the greatest range of options that morally can be justified. Pro-lifers have been particularly involved in efforts to find alternatives to abortion, although this has been unrecognized in the popular press. These efforts need to be redoubled.

If by chance the reader is a woman seeking help in deciding whether to abort her unborn child, she is strongly encouraged to give a pro-life pregnancy counseling center a call before making a final decision (for example: Birthright, USA: toll-free, 1-800-848-LOVE; or Birthright, CANADA: toll-free, 1-800-328-LOVE, or Bethany, USA: toll-free, 1-800-BETHANY). These centers are dedicated to serving the pregnant woman *and* her child, not one *or* the other, and can meet virtually any need the two may have.

Appendix

Religious Objections
to Abortion

What follows is a brief review of some Catholic, Protestant, and Jewish objections to abortion. These arguments are presented because, for most Americans, religious tradition forms the main foundation of their ethical decision-making and epistemological/metaphysical systems. Most of the quotes are taken from the U.S. Senate hearings on abortion during 1974, though additional citations are also added at the end of each subsection for the reader wishing more recent commentaries and opinions.

It should be realized that in each religious tradition there may be spokespersons who champion the pro-life viewpoint and spokespersons who champion the pro-choice viewpoint. In this author's opinion, the arguments presented here are encountered more commonly than any other for the religious tradition being mentioned. Religious traditions that have not taken a consistent pro-life viewpoint (e.g., the Presbyterians and the Reformed Jews) are not presented, even though atypical pro-life spokespersons could be quoted. The religious traditions mentioned include the two largest denominations found in the United States; namely, the Roman Catholic and the Southern Baptist.

Jewish

Rabbi David Bleich, Professor of the Talmud at Stern College, New York, has expressed the following opinion in regard to abortion:

I view the question of permissiveness with regard to the destruction of fetal life as a fundamental moral question rather than as a specifically or uniquely religious question. Western society has long recognized that man's moral conscience bids him to eschew homicide as an offense against morality. Murder is abhorrent to all and the universally recognized ban against the taking of human life is not predicated upon sectarian doctrines. By the same token, opposition to indiscriminate abortion is based on the contention that the unborn fetus is a human being and hence, its destruction is tantamount to homicide or manslaughter.

I would like to emphasize that the position of judaism is that the unborn fetus is to all intents and purposes a person and is entitled to protection of society. . . .

. . . Judaism in particular regards all human life as inviolate. No individual may justifiably take the life of another, other than in the process of self-defense. Fetal life as a form of human life is entitled to the self-same safeguards and protection which society accords to all its members.[1]

Rabbi Bleich notes that under halakhic principles abortion is permissible only to save the life of the mother.[2] He concludes,

A Jew is governed by such reverence for life that he trembles lest he tamper unmindfully with the greatest of all divine gifts, the bestowal or withholding of which is the prerogative of G-d [sic] alone. Although he be master over all within the world there remain areas where man must fear to tread, acknowledging the limits of his sovereignty and the limitations of his understanding. In the unborn child lies the mystery and enigma of existence. Confronted by the miracle of life itself man can only draw back in silence before the wonder of the Lord. . . .[3]

Abraham Bloch has summarized the Jewish view of abortion as follows:

Abortion of a fetus, soon after conception, is an act of aggression prohibited in the Bible (Exod. 21:22–23). According to the Talmud, the killing of a fetus does not constitute murder and is not a capital offense (Sanhedrin 57b). A fetus may be aborted if the mother's life is endangered by the pregnancy (Ohalot 7:6). Abortion for the sake of destroying a defective child is not permissible, unless it is essential to the preservation of the physical and emotional health of the mother.[4]

Thus, although the Jewish position does treat fetal life differently than it treats born life, there is little support for abortion. Some Jewish authors have also spoken of the slippery slope between lax abortion laws and genocide, euthanasia, and abortion for the purpose of providing material for fetal research.[5] Finally, both the Rabbinical Alliance of America (Orthodox) and the Union of Orthodox Rabbis of USA and Canada have taken the strongest possible stance in opposition to abortion.[6]

Roman Catholic

John Cardinal Krol, Archbishop of Philadelphia, speaking for himself and other Catholic officials testifying before the Senate subcommittee in 1974, made statements in regard to the Catholic Church's opposition to abortion, including the following:

> We reject any suggestion that we are attempting to impose "our" morality on others. First, it is not true. Second, it is not possible. The right to life is not an invention of the Catholic Church or any other church. It is a basic human right which must undergird any civilized society. . . . Either we have the same right to speak out on public policy or no one has the right to speak. . . . Medical science has amply documented the humanity of the fetus. There would be no question about the humanity of the unborn except that some wish to kill them.[7]

Vatican Council II taught the following:

> God, the Lord of Life, has conferred on man the surpassing ministry of safeguarding life, a ministry which must be fulfilled in a manner that is worthy of man. Therefore, from the moment of conception life must be guarded with the greatest care while abortion and infanticide are unspeakable crimes.[8]

Franciscus Cardinal Seper and Archbishop Hieronymus Hamer reviewed the historical positions of the Catholic Church throughout the last two centuries and noted that although some differences were seen during the Middle Ages in the extent of church leniency afforded early abortions, ". . . it was never denied at that time that procured abortion, even during the first days, was objectively grave fault."[9] In summarizing the Catholic Church's natural law philosophy, they made the following statement:

> Respect for human life is not just a Christian obligation. Human reason is sufficient to impose it on the basis of the analysis of what a human person is and should be. Constituted by a rational nature, man is a personal subject, capable of reflecting on himself and of determining his acts and hence his own destiny: he is free. . . . In the face of society and other men, each human

being possesses himself; he possesses life and different goods; he has these as a right. . . . The person can be definitively subordinated only to God. Man can never be treated simply as a means to be disposed of in order to obtain a higher end.[10]

Seper and Hamer conclude,

Christ's Church has the fundamental solicitude of protecting and favoring life. She certainly thinks before all else of the life which Christ came to bring: "I have come so that they may have life and have it to the full" (Jn. 10:10). But life at all levels comes from God, and bodily life is for man the indispensable beginning. In this life on earth sin has introduced, multiplied and made harder to bear suffering and death. But in taking their burden upon Himself, Jesus Christ has transformed them: for whoever believes in Him, suffering and death itself become instruments of resurrection.[11]

Southern Baptist

The largest Protestant denomination in the United States, the 15-million member Southern Baptist Convention (SBC) has become more pro-life in recent years, in part as a result of the increase in the denomination's willingness to support a literalist view of the Scriptures. Unlike the Roman Catholic and the Jewish religions, the SBC has no officials whose writings or opinions are binding on the membership. Southern Baptists also have no central hierarchical apparatus that can speak for the denomination as a whole because each church congregation is autonomous. The closest that Southern Baptists come to making denomination-wide statements is during the annual meeting of the SBC, where member churches send representatives (called "messengers") to discuss issues and vote on the budgets of some national agencies and seminaries that are funded by donations from member churches. In the 1989 annual meeting of the SBC, the following typical pro-life resolution was passed:

Whereas, Southern Baptists have historically upheld the sanctity and worth of all human life, both born and pre-born, as being created in the image of God; and Whereas, the messengers to the annual meetings of the Southern Baptist Convention during the past decade have repeatedly reaffirmed their opposition to legalized abortion, except in cases where the mother's life is immediately threatened; and Whereas, the Surpeme Court of the United States in the 1973 *Roe v. Wade* decision, and its progeny, denied the right of the fifty state legislatures and the Congress to protect the pre-born child by law; and Whereas, the Court may now be willing to permit the states and the Congress once again to enact legislation regulating and restricting abortion. Therefore, be it *Resolved,* That we, the messengers of the Southern Baptist Convention, meeting in Las Vegas, June 13–15, 1989, do strongly urge the fifty state legislatures and the Congress to enact legislation to restrict the practice of induced abortion; and Be it further *Resolved,* That we urge the Christian Life Commission and the various state Baptist conventions, and their Christian Life Committees, affiliated with the Southern Baptist Convention actively to promote the passage of such legislation; and Be it finally *Resolved,* That we do reaffirm our opposition to legalized abortion, and our support of appropriate federal and state legislation and/or constitutional amendment which will prohibit abortion except to prevent the imminent death of the mother.[12]

Because those who read the Bible and take it literally believe that they have infallible communication from God, they can reach detailed and absolute conclusions on moral and scientific issues. Hence, because most Southern Baptists would fall into this category, along with other literalist Christian denominations, they can conclude absolutely that the beginning of each individual human life is at conception. This conclusion is determined by reference to the pre-existent Jesus being incarnated at the point of conception (Luke 1:31) and the fact that Jesus was in all ways like other humans (Hebrews 2:17). This enables the Southern Baptists to draw the conclusion from the ancient Scriptures that all humans must begin their lives at the same point as Jesus: conception (fertilization).[13]

Other Denominations

Many other denominations in 1987 were on record as being totally opposed to abortion or opposed to abortions except when the life of the mother is at risk.[14] Listed below are the largest of such denominations, those with a membership of 100,000 or more. An asterisk (*) after a denomination indicates a membership of more than one million.

Apostolic Overcoming Holy Church of God, Assemblies of God*, American Baptist Association (Texarkana, Texas), Baptist Bible Fellowship Missions*, Baptist General Conference, Conservative Baptist Association of America, General Association of Regular Baptist Churches, National Association of Free Will Baptists, Anglican Catholic Church, Polish National Catholic Church of America, Christian and Missionary Alliance, The Christian Congregation, Inc., Christian Reformed Church, Churches of Christ*, Church of God (Indiana), Church of God (Tennessee), Independent Fundamental Churches of America, The Islamic Center*, Jehovah's Witnesses, International Society for Krishna Consciousness*, The American Lutheran Church*, Lutheran Church—Missouri Synod*, Wisconsin Evangelical Lutheran Synod, Church of the Nazarene, The American Carpatho-Russian Orthodox Greek Catholic Church, Greek Orthodox Archdiocese of North and South America*, Orthodox Church in America*, Pentecostal Assemblies of Canada, Pentecostal Holiness Church, Presbyterian Church in America (not to be confused with the Presbyterian Church in the United States or the multi-million-member United Presbyterian Church in the United States of America, which have a more liberal position on abortion restrictions), and United Pentecostal Church International.

Notes

Chapter 2. Ethical Concepts and Common Abortion Arguments

1. Kurt Darr, *Ethics in Health Services Management* (New York: Praeger, 1987), 3–7.

2. Warren Reich, ed., *Encyclopedia of Bioethics,* vol. 1 (New York: Free Press, 1978), 413–29.

3. Jeremy Bentham, *An Introduction to the Principles of Morals and Legislation* (1776), 18, as reprinted in *The Utilitarian* (Garden City, NY: Anchor Books, 1973).

4. See Tom Beauchamp and James Childress, *Principles of Biomedical Ethics,* 2d ed. (New York: Oxford University Press, 1983), 26–32.

5. "Increase in Abortions," *Washington Post,* Nov. 24, 1990.

6. Lisa Koonin, Hani Atrash, Jack Smith, and Merrell Ramick, "Abortion Surveillance, 1986–1987," *MMWR CDC Surveillance Summaries,* 39 (1990): 23–56.

7. Ray Clinebelle, *The Road to Socioeconomic Suicide* (booklet) (Stafford, VA: American Life League, 1990), 4. An ironic future for the liberal politicians who are embracing abortion rights: They will find in that embrace the demise of even the possibility of a welfare state where the needs of the indigent are adequately met by the government, thanks to the taxpayers.

8. Daniel Callahan, *What Kind of Life: The Limits of Medical Progress* (New York: Simon and Schuster, 1990), 79.

9. Ibid., 274 (Table 7); Daniel Callahan has become famous for his books regarding the rationing of care for the elderly. I have previously challenged him in print concerning his position, and at the same time set forth a summary of the tenets of the pro-life movement. I also have noted the irony of the fact (related to the irony mentioned in Note 7) that the generation that endorsed abortion will probably be the generation that is forced to suffer increased pressures for euthanasia. Succeeding generations probably will not be populous enough and productive enough to meet the future welfare needs of the demographically huge generation that has come to maturity in a nation that has ended protections for the unborn. See Gary Crum, "Pro-life Response to Dr. Callahan's *Setting Limits,*" *St. Louis University Law Journal,* 33, no. 3 (1989): 611–16.

10. Jacqueline Kasun, *The War Against Population: The Economics and Ideology of Population Control* (San Francisco: Ignatius Press, 1988), 134.

11. Figures listed previously in this paragraph are taken from *The World Almanac and Book of Facts: 1991* (New York: Pharos, 1990).

12. Julian Simon, *The War on People* (pamphlet) (Stafford, VA: American Life Education and Trust, 1985), 2–3.

13. Quote attributed to A. Jackson, National Center of Child Abuse and Neglect (DHHS), by J. Willke, and J. Willke, *Abortion: Questions and Answers,* 3d ed. (Cincinnati: Hayes Publishing Co., 1990), 145.

14. P. Ney, "Relationship Between Abortion and Child Abuse," *Canadian Journal of Psychiatry* 24 (1979): 610–20, as quoted by Willke and Willke, 146.

15. *The Merck Manual of Diagnosis and Therapy,* 14th ed. (Rahway, NJ: Merck, Sharp and Dohme Research Laboratories, 1982), 1699.

16. Ibid., 1919.

17. For a discussion of this and other facts relative to the court defense of Karl Brandt, the key physician defendant at the Nuremberg medical crimes trial, see Gary Crum, "Nazi Bioethics and a Doctor's Defense," *Human Life Review* 8, no. 3 (1982): 55–69.

18. Merck Manual, 1930–33.

19. Ibid., 1803.

20. Ibid., 1827.

21. For an infamous example of a clinic that specializes in sex-selection ultrasound procedures, see Laura Muha, "Ultrasound Clinic Sparks Controversy," *New York Newsday,* Dec. 2, 1990.

22. For an exhaustive critique of the scientific claim that fetal tissues have been shown to be indispensible for scientific inquiry, see Peter McCullagh, *The Foetus as Transplant Donor: Scientific, Social and Ethical Perspectives* (Chichester, England: John Wiley and Sons, 1987).

23. Ibid.

24. Ibid.

25. John Arras and Robert Hunt, *Ethical Issues in Modern Medicine,* 2d ed. (Palo Alto, CA: Mayfield Publishing, 1983), 16.

Chapter 4. Science and Personhood

1. William May, "Abortion and Man's Moral Being," in *Abortion Pro and Con,* ed. Robert Perkins (Cambridge, MA: Schenkman Publishing Co., 1974), 22.

2. Clifford Bajema, *Abortion and the Meaning of Personhood* (Grand Rapids, MI: Baker Book House, 1974), 84. (Emphasis in the original.)

3. Joseph Fletcher, "Indicators of Humanhood: A Tentative Profile of Man," *The Hastings Center Report* 2, no. 5 (1972): 1–4.

4. Michael Tooley, "Abortion and Infanticide," *Philosophy and Public Affairs* 2 (1972): 41–42.

5. Michael Tooley, *Abortion and Infanticide* (Oxford, England: Clarendon Press, 1983), 421.

6. Daniel Callahan, *Abortion: Law, Choice and Morality* (New York: Macmillan, 1970), 291.

7. Ibid.

8. Baruch Brody, *Abortion and the Sanctity of Human Life: A Philosophical View* (Cambridge, MA: MIT Press, 1975), 87.

9. Richard Werner, "Abortion: The Moral Status of the Unborn," *Social Theory and Practice* 3 (Fall 1974): 218.

10. James Hanick, *Persons, Rights, and the Problem of Abortion* (Ann Arbor, MI: University Microfilms, 1975), 120.

11. *Roe v. Wade,* 410 U.S. 113 (1973), 159.

12. Ibid., 158.

13. Ibid., 162.

14. For two comprehensive critiques of the historical analysis used by the Supreme Court in *Roe v. Wade*—in particular a discussion of how the Court failed to examine adequately the legal and historical precedents that plainly show the welfare of the unborn was not subordinate to the safety of the mother in the development during the mid-1800s of more stringent abortion laws throughout the United States—see R. Byrn, "An American Tragedy," *Fordham Law Review* 41 (1973): 807–39; and J. Dellapenna, "The History of Abortion: Technology, Morality, and Law," *University of Pittsburgh Law Review* (1979): 359–428. For a discussion of how *Roe v. Wade* was indeed an example of how the Supreme Court overstepped its constitutional powers, see the following two constitutional law apologists who seldom agree on much else concerning *Roe v. Wade*: Robert Bork, *The Tempting of America: The Political Seduction of the Law* (New York: Simon and Schuster, 1990), 115–16; and Laurence Tribe, *Abortion: The Clash of Absolutes* (New York: W. W. Norton, 1990), 110.

15. Roger Wertheimer, "Understanding the Abortion Argument," in *The Rights and Wrongs of Abortion,* eds. Marshall Cohen, Thomas Nagel, and Thomas Scanlon (Princeton University Press, 1974), 38. This work by Wertheimer was originally published as an article by the same title in the first issue of *Philosophy and Public Affairs* (Fall, 1971).

16. J. C. Willke, and (Mrs.) J. C. Willke, *Abortion: Questions and Answers,* 3d ed. (Cincinnati: Hayes, 1990), 24.

17. Brody, 84.

18. Kristin Luker, *Abortion and the Politics of Motherhood* (Berkeley: University of California Press, 1984), 180 (emphasis is in the original). See also Lisa Cahill, "Abortion, Autonomy, and Community," in *Abortion: Understanding Differences,* eds. Sidney Callahan and David Callahan (New York: Plenum, 1984), 261–76. For a contrast to these pro-choice viewpoints, see Stuart Kolner, "The Superimposition of Being: The Collision of Maternal and Fetal Rights," *The Pharos* (Spring, 1990): 34–37.

19. Wertheimer, 38.

20. K. D. Whitehead, *Respectable Killing: The New Abortion Imperative* (New Rochelle, NY: Catholics United for the Faith, Inc., 1972), 50.

21. Hans-Martin Sass, "Brain Life and Brain Death: A Proposal for a Normative Agreement," *Journal of Medicine and Philosophy* 14, no. 1 (1989): 45–59.

22. Brody, Chapter 7, passim.

23. Ibid., 107.

24. Paul Ramsey, *The Patient as Person* (New Haven, CT: Yale University Press, 1970), passim.

25. Brody, 83.

26. Andre Hellegers, Filmed interview in *Morality of Abortion* (collection of videotape interviews), eds. Thomas Cox and Thomas Syzek, #AD 11, Georgetown University Library, Washington, D.C., undated.

27. John Dedek, *Human Life: Some Moral Issues* (New York: Sheed and Ward, 1972), 69.

28. Callahan, 389.

29. Brody, 91.

30. Ibid., 114.

31. Roger Wertheimer, "Philosophy on Humanity," in Perkins (Note 1), 121.

32. Paul Ramsey, "The Morality of Abortion," in *Life or Death: Ethics and Options* (Seattle: University of Washington Press, 1968), as reported in Callahan, 379–80.

33. Hanick, 27.

34. Willke and Willke, 39.

35. Pearl Buck, Foreword to *The Terrible Choice: The Abortion Dilemma*, eds. Robert Cooke, et al. (Toronto: Bantam Books, 1968), x.

36. Paul Ramsey, "Points in Deciding About Abortion," in *The Morality of Abortion: Legal and Historical Perspectives*, ed. John Noonan, Jr. (Cambridge: Harvard University Press, 1970), 67.

37. Callahan, 339.

38. Ibid.

39. Dedek, 17–18.

40. Brody, 89.

41. Benjamin Brawley, *A Social History of the American Negro* (New York: Macmillan, 1921; reprinted, New York: Johnson Reprint Corp., 1968), 131.

42. Howard Schuman, C. Steeh, and L. Bobo, *Racial Attitudes in America: Trends and Interpretations* (Cambridge, MA: Harvard University Press, 1985), 9.

43. Richard Burkey, *Racial Discrimination and Public Policy in the United States* (Lexington, MA: Heath Lexington Books, 1971), 19–20; and Ronald Reagan, *Abortion and the Conscience of the Nation* (Nashville, TN: Thomas Nelson Publishers, 1984), 19.

44. For an insightful study of the parallels between the treatment of the unborn in the United States and the treatment of the Jews during the Nazi period, see William Brennan, *The Abortion Holocaust* (St. Louis: Landmark Press, 1983), especially 49 and 104; but for a discussion of the limitations of the Nazi analogy in judging current policies, see Gary Crum, "The Nazi Analogy in Bioethics," *The Hastings Center Report* 18 (Aug./Sept. 1988): 31.

45. See Werner, 203–4; Werner challenges this argument by pointing out that it would permit one to kill someone who is experiencing a period of temporary loss of brain function because the hapless human being so killed would not be a "person." This is because he or she obviously did not achieve the last qualification of Brody's: a functioning brain *in the future*. (Author's note: This may seem to be an over-specific and harsh interpretation of Brody's position, until it is realized that he would permit the killing by abortion of developing human embryos who were not allowed time to obtain the same type of functioning.)

46. A recent report on fetal viability—*Fetal Extrauterine Survivability* (Report of the Committee on Fetal Extrauterine Survivability to the New York State Task Force on Life and the Law, January, 1988)—concluded that "in the foreseeable future, it is likely that technological advances in the care of newborns . . . will not lower the threshold for fetal extrauterine survival" (12). The phrase "foreseeable future" is a key one and is used often in this report to qualify the pessimistic outlook the experts saw for moving the point of viability back to earlier than 24 weeks. It seems to this author that it is quite possible that in the more distant future an artificial womb or umbilicus could be invented or perhaps a practical method could be invented for using the new oxygenated fluids as lung instillations for newborns. It displays a poor respect for the history of scientific advance to say that such developments could never take place.

47. Homeostasis, a concept coined by Harvard physiologist Walter Bradford Cannon, refers to the "self-regulation by living organisms to maintain a constant norm" (Isaac Asimov, *The Intelligent Man's Guide to Science, Vol. 2, The Biological Sciences* (New York: Basic Books, 1960), 728. Although it can be said that the developing human embryo exhibits homeostasis, it is not true of, say, the dead or dying adult human being who has some minor

tissues still functioning. The death of the individual human organism, that is, the reaching of the point where homeostasis is no longer exhibited, precedes the point where every cellular subunit of the organism has ceased to exhibit life. One reason to move toward a brain-death definition of death is to give some legal justification for removing the organs of the brain-dead for transplantation. One way of looking at the living qualities of the legally (supposedly) dead person whose organs are being removed is to ask why we never transplant organs from people who died and were buried several years ago. The answer is because their organs are biologically dead, not just legally dead: The cellular components of those tissues have irreparably ceased to be capable of metabolism and of contributing to the homeostasis-maintenance needs of another human organism.

48. Lynton Caldwell, *Biocracy: Public Policy and the Life Sciences* (Boulder, CO: Westview Press, 1987), 100. Caldwell attempts to draw a distinction between "life" and "a life," which parallels the homeostasis argument.

49. Hanick, 50.

50. Dedek, 72.

51. Wertheimer, "Understanding the Abortion Argument," 27.

52. Ibid., 33–34.

53. Ibid., 50.

Appendix

1. *Hearings Before the Subcommittee on Constitutional Amendments, U.S. Senate, 93rd Congress, Abortion-Part 1.* (Washington, DC: U.S. Government Printing Office, 1974), 287–88.

2. Ibid., 289.

3. Ibid., 305–6.

4. Abraham, Bloch, *A Book of Jewish Ethical Concepts* (New York: Ktav Publishing, 1984), 225–26.

5. For a classic article along this vein, see S. Grumet and F. Rosner, "The Morality of Induced Abortion," *Jewish Life* 38 (1971). 5–12.

6. T. Bosgra, *Abortion, The Bible and the Church* (Toronto: Life Cycle Books, 1987), 32.

7. *Hearings . . .* , 155.

8. *Gaudium et Spes,* 51, 1966, as quoted in *Excerpt from Human Life in Our Day, Pastoral Letter, National Conference of Catholic Bishops,* November, 1968 (included in Ibid., 251).

9. Card. Seper, and H. Hamer, *Declaration on Procured Abortion* (Boston: Daughters of St. Paul DSP Pamphlet PM0510, undated), 9.

10. Ibid., 11–12.

11. Ibid., 22–23.

12. Gary Crum, *Southern Baptists and Abortion Policy* [Castello Institute Medical Ethics Policy Monograph], (Stafford, VA: Anastasia Books, 1989), 26–27.

13. For further discussion of the literalist/fundamentalist viewpoint and Bible verses relating to the abortion issue, see Gary Crum, "Fundamentalists and Abortion," *New Oxford Review* 55(6): 16–21.

14. Bosgra, 28–35.

Section Two

Pro-Choice, Pro-Family, and Pro-Empowerment

Chapter 1

Introduction

A bortion is a medical procedure, a demographic trend, a legal issue, and a political policy issue. Above all else, however, it is a symbol—a symbol of death to its opponents, of freedom of choice to its proponents; a symbol of family responsibility to one group, of a woman's privacy to another; of the state's right to control reproduction, of the state's encroachment on rights adhering in the individual. If we look to other countries we can find a growing public concern about population—declining rates of fertility in some places, increasing rates of fertility in others, and, in many of the developed countries, growing interest in the social impact of large, aging populations. Yet nowhere is there anything comparable to the clash of opinion and the intensity of feeling engendered by the politics of abortion and reproductive rights that has taken place in the United States. It is, then, a peculiarly American controversy. The drama being enacted in the news media, legislatures, courts, churches and synagogues, classrooms, bedrooms, and on the streets is, in reality, about American society: what it ought to be, what it was, and what it is becoming.

The American debate about abortion—whether it is morally and legally right or wrong, the methods of abortion and conditions for either permitting or mandating it—did not start with the United States Supreme Court decision of 1973, *Roe v. Wade*, or with the feminist movement. Philosophers, theologians, law-makers, economists, and ordinary people who have thought about the family at all have also reflected on abortion, contraception, and infanticide. Their views, which are widely diffused through the popular press and the media generally, are seldom integrated and may go past each other without notice. But this patchwork pattern of

69

contradictory opinions and beliefs is an accepted reality in open societies where uniformity is neither feasible nor desirable.

What gives the current debate its unique character is the convergence of three powerful ideas: gender equality, the concept of individual choice, and a belief in planning. The combination of these ideas is quintessentially American, but carries within it three independent flash points, each one of which has its own countercharge. Inequality, national purpose, and competition are also part of our social, economic, and political history, and they, too, elicit loyalties. When historians write the history of the last half of the 20th century, their story will not be about abortion, but about the status of women, about the way we, as a nation, balanced privacy and individual choices with societal priorities, about the mix of state planning and deregulation, and about a monopolistic economy with a belief in the market economy governed only by an invisible hand. Abortion is simply part of the *mise-en-scène*.

The new field of applied ethics and the new professional group of bioethicists have attempted to bring some order into this confused, tense situation by using their broader and more detached philosophical knowledge to referee the debates, negotiate the differences, and act as peacekeepers. But their ethical perspectives, although welcome, are not above the battle; their biases are those of ethical traditions that judge the conduct of individuals while ignoring the behavior of social institutions. Kantian or utilitarian, they are bedside philosophers who with great understanding and compassion often use traditional ethics to comfort and guide individuals who face moral dilemmas. Some go beyond bedside counseling to propose that these solutions based on individual cases be included in debates on social policy. But, in the end, they define as individual, private, and moral the problems that others define as social, public, and political. Indirectly, without intending it, they may blame the victim so that they can help her. Their views, then, must be examined as skeptically as those of the partisans.

Three Key Ideas: Gender Equality, Choice, and Planning

Gender equality

Although the partisans and spokespersons may be men, the subject is women and their reproductive choices. The changing status of women since World War I has been well documented. In the 1920s the successful campaign for women's suffrage created an expectation of participation in public life, while urbanization, education, and industrialization led to smaller, more mobile families. A growing white-collar economy in both the public and private sectors provided new opportunities for employment and the upward mobility of women. Women benefited as well from the welfare state. Starting with the Great Depression and developing more fully during and following World War II, the welfare state inscribed onto the template of American life concepts of social insurance that took much of the uncertainty out of a cyclical boom–bust economy. In the process the American woman was transformed from an over-protected, Victorian, home-bound dependent to a mid-20th-century social and political person, a risk-taking, responsible partner; from "the angel in the house" to the working mother.

The angel in the Victorian household, a paragon of virtue "whose goodness, purity, chastity and religion have so often and deservedly been the theme of poets," was also cunning and shrewd. Writing in 1871, a physician warns his colleagues and husbands to be alert:

As society now looks upon this sin [abortion], we must always be on our guard. Wives will even make the hazardous attempt to keep both husband and physician in ignorance of the procured abortion.[1]

The contemporary woman has a different image. Though far from perfect, she shares with men that capacity to make judgments and assume responsibility.

In this 20th-century environment, gender relations acquired new forms while the meaning of the terms *male* and *female, feminine* and *masculine*, were contested. Marriage and motherhood were similarly being revised by divorce, voluntarily childless families, dual careers, and children's rights. Sexual activity became separate and distinct from procreative sex, and both became separate and distinct from marriage. These two developments culminated in the "sexual revolution" of the 1960s and posed a serious threat to the "moral majority" and to all who believed in premarital chastity, the sanctity of the traditional family, and the special role of women as mothers and homemakers. Pro-life groups were recruited from the ranks of people who wanted to turn the sexual revolution back, to restore the pre-eminence of procreative sexuality, and to restrain by law, if necessary, the control of women over their own sexuality and childbearing. "The woman's right to the sovereign control of her own body ends," one pro-life writer says, "when she consents to intercourse."[2]

A woman consents to intercourse, however, in a social context. At the turn of the century and in a labor-intensive agricultural economy, her consent was driven by the imperatives of the economy. By the end of the century the pressures to have large families had greatly diminished, but the ethos of pro-natalism remained and haunted couples who chose not to have children. They were and are still constantly put on the defensive, called upon to explain what is perceived as "unnatural." The reasons imputed to them are medical (sterility), moral (selfishness), and psychological (unconscious fear of adult responsibility, of childbirth, and so forth), reasons that reflect our distrust of change, our resentment about the freedom enjoyed by such couples, and above all our reluctance to believe that women can find any other identity besides motherhood.

The justifications given by childless couples are similar to those that pregnant women must give to terminate a pregnancy. They, too, are often seen as selfish or neurotic, or both. Neither the pregnant woman nor her counterpart who wishes to remain childless understands why her decision must be approved while the decision to have children does not because the latter has far greater consequences for the community. Despite all the changes taking place in our social structure, then, we are still pro-family and continue to think of reproduction within a medical model. These are some of the longer-lasting biases of our culture that we are not always aware of. They explain why the abortion debate takes place in an environment that is not neutral; if it is not pro-natal it is pro-adoption, pro-contraception, and pro-expert.

As for the sexual revolution, it was never as radical as its critics claimed. Men still took the initiative in sexual activity, and women still bore the major responsibility for setting the limits to sexuality and childbearing; women were and still are blamed when things go wrong, when couples who want children are unable to have them (infertility), and when couples who do not want children do have them. Sexual intercourse itself, which we think of as being driven by natural hormones, is structured around gender inequality. Rape and incest are the extreme examples of coercion, but for many women sex is a "conjugal duty." It may be a pleasure as well as a duty, but the woman may have no choice about the time or place. Thus, what is for men an *expressive* act is for women an *instrumental* one.

The following example illustrates the pseudo-consensual nature of intercourse. A woman in her late twenties had been having an affair with a man who eventually went to Vietnam. By the time he returned, the relationship had cooled off on both sides; nevertheless, when he returned for his first visit, she reported,

> I felt real obligated to sleep with him again even though I hadn't taken any pills. I mean, my God, he's gone off and gotten shot at, and I really felt I had

to give him the American Welcome home. So I did it, though I really didn't want to. I remember just shutting my eyes and breathing a lot and hoping he couldn't tell.[3]

In short, the sexual revolution that took the guilt out of sex retained the asymmetrical relationship between men and women.

The covering ideology of this revolution was equality, and the trend in our thinking about the relationship between men and women was toward greater equality and partnership. The goal was to make the ideology a reality, to legitimate fully what was partially legitimated. What lagged behind was the institutionalization of these trends, for what was a goal for women was often perceived as a threat by men; what was justice to one was reverse discrimination to the other. In practice, then, gender equality remains an unfulfilled promise in American life. Abortion is one way women have tested its limits.

Choice

American public opinion is pro-choice and, with small fluctuations, has been for more than two decades. Among Catholics as well as Protestants, black women as well as white, the percentage who oppose all forms of abortion is negligible (Blake 1973). Men's support for abortion is slightly stronger than women's, but women medical students are considerably more in favor of abortion than men students (Rodman et al. 1987). Approval, however, is not unconditional, and many people who think it should be legal may also disapprove of it on moral grounds or accept it for other people but not for themselves. There is still fear of abuse, a fear masking a latent distrust of reason in the area of human emotions. Nevertheless, during the past two decades the trend to support pro-choice has remained supportive despite the statements of two presidents (Reagan and Bush) and the efforts of Pope John Paul II, Mother Teresa, and television's evangelical preachers.

Support for abortion is strongest for categories where women are victims of rape or incest, where there is evidence of fetal deformity, and where the health or life of the pregnant woman is in jeopardy; it is weakest when women are more agential, deciding for themselves ("a poor woman who feels she cannot afford another child"). It is stronger among working women and weaker among black women who come from large families (McCormick 1975). Still, these statistics about attitudes toward abortion should be viewed with caution. Attitudes measured in the late 1960s and early 1970s may be a reaction to the pro-natalism of the baby-boom years as parents discovered the high costs of educating children born in that period. A second caveat is that right-to-life groups and their followers may be fewer in number but may feel more strongly about the abortion issue than do suppporters of pro-choice. Nevertheless, even after discounting for some of the methodological problems in different studies, the statistics indicate, as so many other surveys in the past have, that public opinion is more liberal than that of politicians and elected officials.

Public opinion reflects the activities of pro-choice and feminist movements that have attempted to influence and mobilize opinion. Membership in these movements overlaps, but the movements can also be seen as having different histories. Catholics for a Free Choice owes more to liberation theology than to feminism. Other pro-choice groups are rooted in the older family-planning movement that became a catalyst in the rapidly declining birthrate. They, too, may dissent from many of the political goals in the feminist program. The feminist emphasis on the principle of choice links contraception, abortion, and the use of the new reproductive technologies, and these, in turn, are regarded as the necessary, although not sufficient, conditions for gender equality. Working together these groups have influenced each other, but it is important to recognize that there is not one pro-choice position; there are several. Analytically, we can distinguish between pro-abortion and pro-choice; the former is a single issue within a health and family planning model; the latter is a broader, more political view on the relationship between gender and justice.

At the margin between pro-choice and anti-choice is the debate among black activists and many third-world leftist groups about the function of birth control and abortion. Unlike the third world where family planning was often initiated by the military or right-wing governments in power as a means of dealing with poverty, Black Power groups in the United States were not opposing reactionary governments; nevertheless, they were suspicious of programs initiated by white middle-class women. Pro-choice, according to Wright (1969), is part of the white supremacy model and a way of maintaining, through numbers, the power of whites. Responding to this, Hudgins saw a better political future for blacks in family planning. "Mao has said freedom comes out of the barrel of a gun," he says. "I have yet to hear someone say freedom comes out of a womb."[4]

For black women, particularly poor women, one of the major abuses suffered was involuntary sterilization (Davis 1983). White male doctors, federal officials, and local judges often saw no violation of human rights in ordering sterilization for young black women who if they had to choose between involuntary motherhood and involuntary infertility might prefer the former. These women are passively pro-choice where abortion is concerned and actively opposed to the denial of freedom in forced sterilization, but their politics are shaped primarily by everyday bread-and-butter issues.

Similarly, there is diversity on the other side. Opponents of pro-choice have often been opponents of birth control in any form, and they have achieved some success politically to have sex education in schools canceled and funding for family-planning clinics cut off. But these are small incremental steps in an unending campaign to protect the traditional family and its religious foundations. Other anti-choice groups emphasize contraception as a form of prevention and limit their criticism to abortion, the destruction of life. A critical test of their strength came in 1970 when the state of Washington held a referendum on abortion (Fujita and Wagner 1973). Months of lobbying preceded the vote and voter turnout was heavy; but when the day was over, pro-choice groups had a major victory: 56.5 percent in favor of the referendum; 43.5 percent against it.

The Washington referendum experience brought Catholic nuns and women well past the age of menopause together in a joint support of pro-choice. No one could say that biological self-interest was the motivation for their presence and militant support. Indeed, the ethos of the new institutional or social structural equality emphasized what these two categories of women may have missed in their lives: personal choice. Deeply entrenched in the American mind and, indeed, in Western civilization, the right to choose has never been spread equitably across class, race, or gender. Nevertheless, the right to choose remains a commitment, an idea that commands loyalty and can mobilize people into social action.

The origin of our Western concept of choice lies in modern politics as well as in modern science and technology. Modern politics gave us a concept of freedom based on volition, on the absence of coercion, and the ability of individuals to make rational decisions. Modern science and technology freed us from the rigid and harsh necessities of nature. Ecologists today look at this trend with some degree of alarm and question whether a better life could have been achieved for more people if our efforts to overcome nature had been slower and more sensitive to the rhythms of nature. Many of the critics of modern medicine and its application to reproduction rejoice, on the one hand, in the notion that sickness and health are not inevitable, that patients and physicians have choices, but deplore, on the other hand, the loss of affective caring in high technology. The new challenge is not in nature but in social life. Over time, and not without conflict and opposition, we have extended the principle of choice first to religion in the 17th century, to government and politics in the 18th century, and to consumption and the marketplace in the 19th century. In the 20th century we have applied it to the organization of work and the family. Thus, the term *pro-choice* does not refer to the advocacy of abortion but to the democratization of the family. It includes the choice of couples to have large families, small families, or no families.

Within these broad parameters, the pro-choice position posits a legal environment that permits abortion and protects women from harassment; it means access to abortion through established medical services, hospitals, or clinics without discrimination based on age, class, or race. Above all, pro-choice means the freedom to feel morally right about oneself.

Having the right to make a choice, however, should not be confused with the process of decision making. The ideal of making wise or informed choices is a value against which we measure decision-making performance, our own and that of others. Freedom of choice may be instrumental to other ends or an end in itself, but it is a fundamental principle of a free society and places the burden of proof on those who deny it. In 1966, for example, the United Nations issued a document on population that began with the statement that "the size of the family should be the free choice of each individual family." A few years later the United Nations spelled it out again, saying that "couples have the basic human right to decide freely and responsibly on the number and space of their children, and the right to adequate education in this respect."[5]

The psychology of decision making is a different matter. We have only to look at our electoral decisions to realize how often they represent a mix of rationality and irrationality, wisdom and foolishness, to realize how we confuse the image with the person and how often we vote for the right party for the wrong reasons and for the wrong party for the right reasons. Nonetheless, we affirm the right of a citizen in a democracy to make a choice, to vote and to speak out on public issues.

The same set of mixed motives and imperfect decision making occurs in family life as well. Deciding whether to have an abortion is difficult, particularly if it is a woman's first pregnancy. Making the decision is even more agonizing when the women is young, unmarried, and living at home. It is a major crisis in her young life for which she has no preparation and few role models. Her support system of peers may be just as immature and inexperienced as she is: "My friend says she takes her friend's pills. Another says she takes her grandmother's pills. Bullshit. What would a grandmother need with birth-control pills? You can't believe nobody."[6] Indeed, experienced professional counselors may be nearly as overwhelmed (Joffe 1986), "affective neutrality" notwithstanding.

The options open to a pregnant girl—adoption, abortion, raising a child—are all perceived as negative: "I did not want another fatherless child."[7] Many women reject the option of adoption because, in their minds, giving up a child for adoption is immoral whereas abortion is merely illegal. "I'm too maternal to carry a baby for nine months," a 19-year-old woman says, "and give it up for adoption. I couldn't bear giving it away like a toy."[8] Another woman who considered adoption described it as "giving them away like they're a bag of garbage or something."[9] "Carrying the child for nine months and allowing it to be born seemed much more unnatural than aborting a fetus I hated."[10] "I have no other choice. The abortion will be better than having the baby and then giving it up. I've been through foster homes myself, and I couldn't do that to another person."[11] "I don't believe in kids being orphans and stuff. They grow up wondering why their parents didn't want them and all that."[12]

These excerpts convey some sense of how pregnant women reflect on the alternatives available. They decline to express any criticism of the social structure that offers them so little choice; at the same time, the legal and ethical questions about abortion raised by theologians, legal theorists, ethicists, and other moral experts are strange and remote from their lives.

But critics of abortion are often right when they say that "abortion is experienced not as an act of 'choice' but as an act of despair—their *only* choice"[13] (Reardon 1987).

> I wouldn't have this abortion if I didn't have to, but I can't support a child and I can't take it to where the father is. If the father of the baby was here and if he would marry me, I wouldn't have this abortion. I don't know how I'm going to settle it with my conscience, but I'm going to have to because I can't have this baby.[14]

If Reardon is right that abortion is an act of despair, it is difficult to see how prohibiting abortion would, in any way, lessen the anguish. Among those who reject abortion and have live births, a very small number (four percent) opt for adoption, despite efforts by pro-natalist doctors, pro-family religious leaders, pro-pregnancy psychiatrists, and other intervenors. Women with a strong sense of their future handle the decision with fewer emotional upheavals (Zimmerman 1977), but it is almost always a decision about which there is a lifetime of doubt and often debilitating residues of regret.

Studies of the decision-making process, however, provide us with the best information we have about the way women think about issues of reproduction. Any woman, young or old, who is unwillingly pregnant and feels she has a choice to make becomes her own ethicist as she makes her way through all of the messages that demographers, religious leaders, social workers, feminists, and pro- and anti-natalists have directed to her. It is the woman making her rational choice who provides us with the propositional foundation for a woman-centered reproductive ethic.

Planning

If choice is a very American value, so is planning. We do not believe in just letting things happen, or the forces of destiny. We plan our economic production and distribution, our cities and school systems, and would, if we could, plan the weather. In the absence of information as a basis of planning, we would rather gamble than drift, take our chances rather than passively let events happen. Planning the number of children and their spacing in a family is part of growing-up in America; boys as well as girls have an image of their ideal family long before they are likely to need to do anything to ensure that the plan is realized. Implicit in our socialization is the idea that deciding whether to have no children or several, whether the children should follow close together or be spread apart, is the responsibility of individuals, not the state. Responsible family planning means finding the right kind of contraception and learning how to use it and figuring out what to say and do in the event that a partner does not cooperate. Planning also means deciding how to handle contingencies, what would or could be done in the event that the contraceptive device is forgotten or fails. Thus, the pregnancy that is terminated is typically the unplanned one, more unplanned than undesired. One woman may want to complete her education before starting a family; another woman may feel she has completed her family. Both women resent that these reasons are not sufficient for justifying an abortion and that they are forced to enter into a series of lies and deceptions, sometimes coached by their own physicians on what to say to a hospital committee that must approve their application to terminate the pregnancy. Who can say that their decision to terminate the pregnancy is not a rationalization of a deeper unconscious rejection by the women of parenthood? But the notion that a planned family will be more fulfilling for parents and better for children is well established in the professional literature and the folklore of family life.

Family planning in our society is a mix of folk knowledge and modern research-based medicine. The latter is, in turn, dependent on a developed pharmaceutical industry and sophisticated hospital delivery systems. The pharmaceutical industry and hospital system are the unplanned sector of American life, left to entrepreneurial initiative and a market model of competition. The United States stands alone in this respect, for its neighbor Canada and most European countries have moved toward health care systems that are planned and reflect the concepts of social justice incorporated in the welfare state. The American debate, then, on the health care system, on the future of a fee-for-service delivery, and on the status of physicians forms part of the background in the debate on reproduction.

Given these trends and countervailing trends, texts and subtexts, it is not surprising that the abortion debate is over-heated and, in Althuserrian terms, over-determined. But in addition to these differences are the profound differences in the way we approach social problems. Some people look at them from a moralistic, judgmental perspective; others look at them from a therapeutic, health one. Each of these differs from the political, liberationist perspective. Pro-life advocates have drawn primarily from the religious and moral tradition. Physicians, social workers, and family planning groups have built their case on the health model, and feminists have focused on a concept of rights. These are not, of course, air-tight compartments. Individuals may often internalize all of them, whereas many groups cross lines. But in general, we can see in the abortion colloquies these different modalities of thought.

Finally, the abortion debate raises questions about law and morality. To what extent can or should law regulate morality, and to what extent should the state encroach on the personal liberty of individuals in a free and democratic society? What do we do in a society based on rule of law that has abortion laws that are demonstrably unenforceable? Law enforcement is crucial, for if we decide as a society that to terminate a pregnancy is a woman's decision, it must be a decision she can make without fear of legal penalty or intrusion on her private space.

Elective abortion, then, has become a code word for other schisms in American life. At some point, however, abortion must be taken literally, not as a symbol for something else. Here, too, there is an irony. Abortion may be very high on the political and judicial agendas and very central for religious elites, but not for the general public for whom other issues have displaced it. The interest curve can be seen by looking back in time. During the first half of the century, before World War II, an unwanted pregnancy, either before or after marriage, was a personal crisis and abortion a social crime. But for many women it was a victimless crime. Once done, it was kept secret and remained on the conscience of the woman forever. *Confession* magazines built their circulations on stories that dwelt on the confessions of women about their transgressions and the price they paid in self-respect for their shame and hidden pasts.

Confessional narratives are still popular, but the *mea culpas* now are more psychological than moral. The next generation made its decisions about abortion more freely, with less concern about lawbreaking and more concern about mental health. The advice they received from psychiatrists, social workers, sex educators, and enlightened parents was as confusing as ever: You were damned if you did, and damned if you didn't. Francke (1978), whose study is more anecdotal than systematic, claims that, in almost all the cases she studied, the aftershock of abortion was damaging. Relationships between single people inevitably broke up, and the women who did not become man-haters became promiscuous. Zimmerman (1977) found a similar pattern, but she also found that certain relationships were strengthened.

The generation reaching puberty today has a different outlook based more on its concern about acquired immune deficiency syndrome (AIDS). "Safe sex" has a priority formerly given to birth control by sex educators. Abortion has also diminished in importance as policy-makers, bioethicists, women's organizations, doctors, and scientists confront infertility and the new reproductive technologies. If we support choice in procreation, contraception, and abortion, do we also support choice in surrogate parenting, *in vitro* fertilization, and embryo transfer? Indeed, in the future what we may see is what recently took place in Britain when an abortion rider (reducing the period when abortion was permissible) was tacked on to a bill mainly concerned with the use of embryos and fetal tissue for purposes of research.[15]

In short, Americans address the question of abortion today with a different framework from that of our Victorian predecessors and our contemporaries in the older European countries and the newer ones in the third world. American women have a different status and a different agenda based on America's historical values of equality and individualism; we have made retaining the right of choice a condition of marriage and of family life—the sexuality of partners, the duration of the marriage, the number of children or whether there are children at all. And we have expressed our deepest belief that we have some control over our lives, that we can and should anticipate the future and plan.

Is there some grand ethical system, some set of universal moral propositions that can deal with contraception, abortion, AIDS and other sexually transmitted diseases, and *in vitro* fertilization? I am going to suggest—and because I am not a trained philosopher I can afford to make these bold statements—that they do constitute a package. A critical reader may conclude, however, that abortion is not an ethical question at all, but rather a social problem that can be dealt with intelligently, wisely, and humanely without resorting to criminal law or moral exhortations. The high rates of teenage pregnancy and abortion, for example, could be reduced through better social planning, by giving young people, especially those who are black or Hispanic and poor, some sense of an economic future, some vision of a society other than the barrios and black inner-city ghettos. Yet, even social problems involve values. To the extent it is appropriate, reproductive control should be considered in the framework of applied ethics. How we resolve the question of the right to terminate a pregnancy, however, does not depend on ethical questions alone; ethics is but one component of a larger social and legal matrix.

If abortion is an ethical question, it is not the same ethical question for women as it is for men. For men, it is a choice between two diametrically opposed positions. For women it is a choice in a ranked order of options. For men it is a question of fetal rights or maternal rights; for women it is the meaning of responsible motherhood. "We could have stretched our finances to absorb yet another family member," one woman said, "but we felt we were unable to stretch our emotional and physical resources, enough to welcome another child."[16] Men and women seldom seem to be addressing the same issues, or addressing them in the same way.

Beyond this there is a more intractable question: Can we make moral decisions in an immoral world? Many of the criticisms people make about abortion are about a society in which our life-chances are governed by a social structure that so constrains us that our right to choose is more shadow than substance. Decisions that appear to be made from choice are within so few degrees of freedom that the choices are, for all practical purposes, made for us before we engage in any reflection on the morality of our choice.

People whose life-chances are better, whose options are wider, people who have good health and economic security and who are able easily to discharge their social obligations are beginning to consider whether in an overpopulated world people are morally obligated to have fewer children than they might wish. A woman who had an abortion, when asked about her decision, said:

> I have never had *one* twinge of guilt or misgiving since I am a devoted
> mother of two, very happy with her lot, who knows there are enough (too
> many) children in the world.[17]

To the extent that the population crisis is the result, not of the distribution of resources, but of there being too many people, reproductive morality goes beyond personal morality. The pro-choice movement, then, should not be confined to the United States or the other wealthy industrialized societies. Pro-choice must be universal, not the luxury of the rich within this country and within the world community. Women in North America do not have pro-choice if women in Brazil do not. The advocacy of procreative choice, then, is on behalf of all women, and is, in turn, linked to international aid and other social policies that close the gap between North and South, the "haves and have-nots." Accordingly, state department policies that cut off funding for any agency in less developed countries that provides abortion or abortion counseling are cruel and insensitive and can only trouble the conscience of women in the United States and elsewhere in the developed world.

In Chapter 2 we look at abortion in three very different contexts: preliterate societies, the Victorian period, and contemporary Eastern Europe. In preliterate societies abortion is widely practiced and without any moral connotation, but is not a choice. Pregnancy may be a crime; abortion is not. Preliterate societies also provide us with an understanding of our own cultural biases about the nature of the fetus and reproduction generally. Victorian society was the origin of the therapeutic model. During this period women had no choice; abortion become criminalized except when doctors permitted it. Victorian society illustrates in the extreme a lesson that we learn from other societies as well: Abortion can be prohibited, but it cannot be prevented. The laws against it are ultimately defeated by the high social costs of enforcing them. The third model is Eastern Europe where, until recently, abortion was not criminal, but also was not a right. There, abortion is not so much a woman's choice but a service provided by the state where other services for family planning are less well developed. In Chapter 3 we focus on teenage abortion and the decision-making process. Teenage pregnancy and teenage abortion touch sensitive nerves in our liberal thinking. Attitudes toward adolescent pregnancy are a barometer of our state of mind about youth, who typically are seen as the most privileged group in our society. They may not be the most privileged, but they are among the most visible, and it is through them that we can see how sexuality is gendered, how men influence the use of contraceptives, how women decide on abortion. They also provide us with some understanding of the limitations of contraception. In the discussion of teenage abortion, we look at three types of counseling: pastoral, family-based social work, and individual family-planning counseling, noting in each a different type of anti-choice bias.

In Chapter 4 we examine the broader models—therapeutic, moral, and legal—and the elites they represent. We shall suggest, then, that there is a fundamental impasse between pro-life and pro-choice groups in the discussions of the fetus; that is, whether we start from the sanctity of fetal life or from the sanctity of the neonatal person is a choice based on faith for there is no scientific or logical basis for the choice. And, indeed, in my view it is the wrong question to be asking, but, in any case, the pro-choice position, whether it is feminist or nonfeminist, rests on a social rather than a medical–biological model of abortion, on priority given to person over fetal life, to relationship over person, and the doctrine of the wanted child. Our critique of the legal model is its assumptions that law is objective and that a group of neutral professionals, trained in mediation skills, can develop a compromise satisfactory to all. In the closing comments, Chapter 5, I state more analytically the pro-choice case, distinguishing between abortion as part of family planning and pro-choice as the empowerment of women in a longer and broader historical perspective.

A note about my own biases. My religious beliefs do not preclude abortion, but I grew up in an era when abortion was criminal. An unwed mother left school and left town, and the child born out of wedlock was labeled and, unless adopted, was avoided socially as if the child carried the bad seed of adultery and sexual indiscretion. Despite state-of-the-art contraception, fear of pregnancy hung over all women despite class, race, or religion. Fear of abortion was just as pervasive and was sustained by third-person reports of terrible pain, surgery with no anaesthetics, unsafe and clandestine environments, police raids, incompetent or sadistic abortionists, hemorrhaging, hospital emergency wards, permanent injury, possible death, and suicides. Any of these scenarios was a deterrent to any kind of healthy, anxiety-free sexuality. The outcome of sexual relations was up to me because men, according to the folk wisdom of an older generation of women, could not, would not, and probably should not have sexual responsibility. Thus, the views expressed here probably reflect a situation that I now, in retrospect, think of as a form of male privilege. Nothing could induce me to turn the clock back. No argument, however elegant in its logical structure, could persuade me that the combination of guilt and fear had any benefits, or that it did anything but cripple women by forcing them to deny their own sexuality.

For a long time I was unsure about where I stood, somewhere between the notions that "abortion should be there if you need it but should not be encouraged, and besides you can count on the state to screw things up" and "abortion should be a contraceptive choice made by women." Indeed, I was not certain of my position until after reading the accounts of women whose reproductive experiences involved abortion, after reading about the cross-cultural and historical development of social attitudes and legislation, and after examining the abstruse discussions of theologians and professors of philosophy. Then I knew where I stood: Abortion should be a contraceptive choice.

Politically, abortion should be a right, not a privilege. But the more I read the more I became aware of two positions: Abortion as part of family social policy, and abortion as a transformative decision (i.e., an act of choice that would alter how I viewed myself as a responsible agent). Either position is regarded as wrong by pro-life activists for whom abortion is abortion is abortion, but it is a question that every woman who is honestly trying to think through the question must confront. For that reason I have given the two positions attention.

Still, I thought, my own position is not realistic. Then I faced a problem we all do. Do the exigencies of history shape our destinies or do we make history? A perceptive reader reading between the lines will surely find traces of my own cultural biography and the intellectual conflicts of the past few months, but these contextual variables, I would maintain, have no bearing on the validity of the ideas.

Chapter 2

Comparative Models

Preliterate: Abortion as Normal

Abortion is widespread throughout preliterate societies and seldom, if ever, proscribed (Devereux, 1968). It is part of maintaining the balance between the number of people and the material resources available. But the limits of material resources are not so fixed that increases or decreases in population always threaten or improve survival, nor do these fluctuations disrupt or destabilize an established social equilibrium. The boundaries are open enough for judgments and choices to be made. Whether they are made by elites and the privileged few or by many, by men or by women, by the young people or the old people, by insiders or by outsiders, is an indicator of other facets of the society; but these key groups define the population issues. Petchesky (1985) distinguishes between population control and birth control; the former is a matter of public policy and the latter is one of individual choice. What we see in noncolonial preliterate societies is primarily population control.

In preliterate societies, reproductive norms concern the choice of partners. A woman whose pregnancy is unacceptable to the community, who has broken its rules about appropriate sexual partners or the number of children—a pregnant widow, an unmarried girl or a girl too young, a women who has had sexual intercourse with an outsider or whose pregnancy is the result of an adulterous relationship—is expected to have an abortion, and she does. These variations reflect different values about the social order and kinship but nothing about abortion itself, for there is no judgment attached to abortion although there may be severe moral judgments passed on the pregnancy and the conditions that led to it.

85

Abortion, however, is not the only way in which societies maintain a population continuity. Contraception and infanticide are as widespread as abortion and may be used more often or regarded as more desirable (Harris and Ross 1987). Abortion may play an important part in some societies, contraception in others, whereas for societies concerned with gender ratios, infanticide is more common (Miller 1981). Nevertheless, cultural anthropologists studying a large and varied range of cultures have found that abortion is the rule rather than the exception (Devereux 1960).

Two observations are relevant to our discussion. The first is the absence of a scientific or medical discourse. In preliterate societies, obstetrical knowledge is a mix of magic and common sense. A spontaneous abortion or miscarriage can be caused by witchcraft, the devil, a co-wife; an induced abortion may be brought about by spells (Devereux 1960). But there is nothing that would correspond to a therapeutic abortion carried out to save the life of the mother.

The second observation is that the fetus is "other," neither human nor inhuman. Some of the depictions of the fetus and what takes place inside the womb may seem bizarre, but the distancing between embryo and woman is a function not of knowledge, but of the family system. The debates among ourselves about when life begins, about whether the fetus is a small human being, about the nature of prenatal bonding, are plausible to us because of our family system in which the child is the biological successor and the social heir whose claims on family affection, attention, and resources are greater than those of other children in the community. Typically, a man thinks of a woman carrying "his" child, and pregnant women have fantasies about the child inside them. Ultrasound imaging has been found to create a bond or to strengthen an existing one between the woman and the fetus (Fletcher and Evans 1983). Women are encouraged to construct very realistic images of a child with whom one can communicate. Oriana Fallaci (1975), the distinguished Italian journalist, describing her own pregnancy and eventual miscarriage, conducts an adult conversation with the imaginary child inside her and decorates her office with enlarged medical pictures intended to make the fetus look human. When she learns the fetus is dead, she puts herself on trial as causing the death of the child by bad thoughts rather than deeds. Following the spontaneous abortion, Fallaci insists on seeing the fetus to which she had bonded, keeping it beside her in a jar. She is shocked to discover the discrepancies between the grey mass in the jar, on the one hand, and, on the other, the enlarged anatomical drawings and the picture in her mind. The fetus in the jar is neither. Daniel Maguire, a Catholic theologian who spent time in an abortion clinic, had a similar experience looking at the tissue. "I have held babies in my hands, and now I held this embryo. I know the difference. This had not been a person or a candidate for baptism."[18] The biological child "belongs" to a woman; its death is a death in the family although the child was never born. The same event would be marked differently in preliterate societies where the biological mother of the child may not be its social mother. The grey mass would represent a different reality. Indeed, it very often does in our own. Women considering abortion talk about "my condition" or "the pregnancy." As one woman expressed it, "I did not think of the thing inside me as a child, but as a problem I wanted to get rid of."[19]

In cultures with different kinship systems and where the status of children is different, gestation is constructed differently. The pregnant woman does not bond or feel a special relationship to the child inside her because her parenting responsibilities may be toward other children. Hence, the disposal of the aborted fetus carries with it no bereavement or death ceremonies; it may be buried in the earth, thrown out, used to fertilize the land, or even consumed as food (Devereux 1960). Again, and it cannot be repeated often enough, these are not simply prescientific ways of thinking; they reflect a social logic as rational as our own. The critical difference is the family system and its relationship to the larger social organization of the society. Believing is seeing, and by believing in the nuclear family we see, through the mediation of language and science, a child, *our* child, in the womb. Other societies believing in other family systems see through their symbolic systems a different entity or may make no connection at all.

Social organization also determines the status of women and their value. Gender-based infanticide demonstrates a preference for males or females, and each sex is valued for different things—men for their bravery; women for their reproductive capacity. A pregnant woman may attempt to abort herself or to seek help from other women, including a midwife. Mothers, sisters, and friends may be with her and assist. But the presence or services of men are seldom required.

Women teach each other their skills of abortion and share their knowledge of abortifacients and pass them on from one generation to the next. In general, an abortion may take place at any time during the pregnancy, from the morning after to the day of delivery; no distinction is made on the basis of "quickening" or "viability." But the methods used, more or less invasive, may vary depending on the stage of gestation. Massage, externally applied ointments, the ingestion of special herbal drinks, suppositories, and internal mechanical manipulation can be found among different peoples (Devereux 1960). Some of the techniques used have become the folk knowledge of our own lives: hot baths, vigorous exercise, tight clothing. Indeed, there may even be some version of the placebo effect. Because we have no reliable records of how well the methods work, of which ones are better than others, or of what the sequences of using them might be, we have to believe the words of informants that they clearly do work and that the confidence women place in them is based on reality.

Medieval reproductive practice is similarly characterized. Folk obstetrics and women-centered practitioners were kept busy despite the theological doctrine that abortion past the stage of *ensoulment*—a concept as supernatural as any found in preliterate societies—was unacceptable (Rowland 1981). Medieval pictorial depictions of the womb resemble the drawings of groups of people on ancient Greek urns. The figures are of human adults playing games and reclining or floating in another world. Midwives knew that what emerged from the womb bore no relation to the visual depictions, but they saw no contradiction or cognitive dissonance, for these were not diagrams of reality. Yet as the family evolved in the postfeudal era our understanding of who and what was in the womb changed. Long before modern obstetrical technology made it possible to study the womb and observe fetal development inside it, the way had been created for our current beliefs regarding the fetus as an extension of ourselves. When miscarriage or stillbirth occurs we are encouraged to mourn the fetus as a deceased member of the family (Borg and Lasker 1982).

The Medieval Woman's Guide to Health is very clear, too, that if a choice arose between saving the fetal life or the mother's, the latter should prevail. Fetal life was not on the same scale as the mother's:

> For when the woman is feeble and the child cannot come out, then it be better that the child be killed than the mother of the child also die.[20]

The benefit of the doubt, then, went to women. Because women were the midwives, it is very likely that liberties were taken in defining the birth as meeting these extreme conditions.

To summarize, abortion in this model carries no particular shame or disapproval, no kudos or approval; it is expected behavior under certain circumstances. Within this framework, the fetus is not regarded as a developing progeny with hereditary kinship ties to the biological mother or father. What is inside the woman's womb is neither human nor inhuman, but simply "other." Women may want their induced abortions to look like spontaneous ones or to blur the distinction. In any case, the methods used incorporate natural components and low technology. Whether successful or not, many of the traditional treatments used in Europe during the Middle Ages to bring on the menstrual period are part of the folklore of women today. However, unlike the women in preliterate societies and of the medieval period, women in our society do not control the knowledge and the distribution of these services.

The fate of the medieval midwives was tragic. As their power and status increased among women, they generated suspicion among men, who eventually accused them of witchcraft. The midwife was one of the victims of persecution by men who claimed she was using the afterbirth for her evil spells. But the tradition of women healers engaged in reproductive activity has never really been extinguished. In recent times, a women's collective in Chicago called "Jane" learned how to carry out abortions in friendly, nonhospital environments and provided a model for demedicalized abortion outside of a hierarchical medical establishment and, incidentally, outside of the law (Jane 1990).

The revolution which took place in Europe during the 16th and 17th centuries—the breakdown of feudalism, the growth of science, the development of the nation state, and the modernization of social and economic structures—took two different directions and resulted in diametrically different approaches to abortion: the Victorian model of criminalization and the legalization of abortion during the Russian Revolution. Ironically, both have reversed themselves to some degree. Socialist countries have outlawed abortion, whereas capitalist countries have moved to legalize it. But these directions are reversible, and it would be a serious error to reduce these historical shifts of the 19th and early 20th century to two competing ideologies.

Victorian: Abortion as Criminal

In preliterate societies, as we have seen, abortion is neither legal nor illegal although the practices are culturally structured. During the Middle Ages, the church spoke out against abortion as a sin after "quickening," but turned a blind eye to the practice itself. Women's healing networks combined a variety of reproductive services, and *The Medieval Woman's Guide to Health* gave, among other things, practical advice on abortion. It was no more secretive about it than it was on infertility treatments. Moreover, it was easier for women to conceal their abortions from the church until after the fact, when they confessed them.

By the 19th century, however, Christianity in all its denominations had become increasingly divided between those who held to orthodox beliefs and reformers who were more secular in their thinking. The abortion question was captured by the conservatives, and abortion, along with contraception and any form of extramarital sex, was condemned in language that combined Calvinist damnation with Catholic guilt. Law followed in the same tradition. Dogma was replaced by case law and statute, but it, too, was tightening up on exceptions and lack of vigilance. A woman who had an abortion could be punished by death. In earlier times if a woman was condemned to death for some crime and she was found to be pregnant, she could escape the death penalty. By the turn of the century, with only limited defense, her life could be taken for having had an abortion. Her best hope was the elimination of capital punishment. The trend from the turn of the century on was toward a vindictive model that made moralists feel self righteous but was, in fact, unenforceable. In 1800 abortion was regulated by English common law and was a misdemeanor. "By 1900," Luker (1984) writes, "every state in the Union had passed a law forbidding the use of drugs or instruments to procure abortion at *any* stage of pregnancy" except where the life of the woman was at risk.[21] These laws punished not only persons who procured the abortion but also women who aborted themselves (Luker 1984).

The advertisements for abortifacients continued, and the laws created an underground system for women to "regulate their periods." The state, which could criminalize abortion, could not enforce it (Mohr 1984). Using patent medicines to self-induce an abortion was the most common practice, but women turned more and more to physicians who shared their views that abortion before quickening was acceptable family practice. The long-term trend to reduce family size coupled with the lack of safe, reliable, convenient contraceptives created a set of cross pressures for young women in their early child-bearing years and made their compliance with the law more difficult. The statistics indicate that married women with children and young married women who wished to delay childbearing were the primary market for abortion services (Mohr 1984) and saw no contradiction between abortion and their own religious beliefs. The same pattern persists today as women compartmentalize their views on abortion and their views on religion (McLaren and McLaren 1986).

Doctors and the public who opposed abortion blamed the trend on too much education making women dissatisfied and causing them to lose respect for the family and their duty. Vanity and selfishness contributed as well. But the rhetoric had little impact, for what the opponents of birth control (contraception and abortion) faced was a more powerful and invisible force: the falling birthrate and a new class structure with smaller, upwardly mobile, middle-class families. Thus, there were show trials of persons who carried out abortions that resulted in the woman's death (Gordon 1974), but there was little serious prosecution. Doctors who were in the forefront of the movement to make abortion illegal were, at the same time, reluctant to make criminal charges against other doctors. In their campaign to make abortion illegal, they inveighed against women and their abettors but seldom, at least in public, mentioned that the so-called abettors were other physicians.

Doctors lost the battle but won the war, for although they did little to prevent women from having abortions, they established their own status as the experts in women's diseases and succeeded in medicalizing such normal processes as pregnancy. At the same time they were finding a niche between the old traditionalism and the new secular religions. But the Victorian physician was not the scientific, "value-free" professional familiar to us. He was a moralist who could denounce "the slaughter of the innocents" with the fervor and moral indignation of an Evangelical preacher; at the same time he was a doctor who saw no contradiction in those two roles. Physicians preached while preachers often healed. What the Victorian physicians achieved, then, was not only a legitimation of themselves as the experts on female disorders, but the displacement of women healers who lacked the qualifications of degrees from medical schools, which they would have been barred from attending, in any case. The criminal abortion law, Davis (1985) writes, was "a symbolic law that embodied the differential status of doctor versus patient and the male professional's total control over decisions regarding women's reproduction."[22] A century later, abortion became legal, but by that time the organization of medicine made it legal for those who could afford the medical system; illegal for those who could not. A dual system of medical care, one for the rich and one for the poor, made safe abortions more accessible to some women than to others.

The Victorian model suggests a number of things. First, the number of women seeking abortions responds to wider trends in population; women risk having abortions not because they are subversive and law-breakers, but because they are part of a generation which is curtailing family size. They find their rationalizations and resolve any cognitive dissonance between normative belief systems and the exigencies of everyday life. Second, the Victorian period marks the beginning of the medical model as a public model, when information about pregnancy was no longer confined to medical school texts and physicians. Everyone was held responsible for the health of the fetus and pregnant woman. Doctors in the 19th century did not talk, as they do today, about having "two patients."

They succeeded in medicalizing the reproductive functions of women and, in addition, wrested control of health care delivery from midwives and from the unlicensed. Third, the prejudices of physicians about women, sexuality, race, and class became institutionalized, in effect triaging poor women into illegal and late abortions and creating a system of social control. As Illsley and Hall put it

> Guilt about abortion has been, and in most countries continues to be, deliberately induced as part of a traditional system of social control. In such circumstances, it is superfluous to ask whether patients experience guilt—it is axiomatic that they will.[23]

Socialist Countries: Abortion as a Social Service

The socialist countries of Eastern Europe provide a different model of reproductive practice, one in which abortion is legal and the medical risks associated with illegal abortions and dubious practitioners are significantly reduced. But although women have choice, they do not have individual rights. Further, although doctors perform the abortions and women are patients, the abortions are not necessarily therapeutic or even necessarily related to the health of the pregnant woman. She is a patient entitled to a medical service in connection with her pregnancy, but pregnancy is not defined as illness. And finally, abortion is available to all without economic discrimination. Access may be difficult and require bureaucratic skills, but no woman is denied an abortion because she is unable to pay for the service because the service is free. Future privatization may change this and create a two-tier system with a differential in the quality of service offered in the private and public clinics; meanwhile, abortion and other related services are available without regard for income differences.

Lenin made abortion legal in the Soviet Union during the early days of the Revolution as part of a new freedom for women. Stalin, however, reversed the policy and when in 1955 abortion became legal again, the earlier feminist ideology had dropped out. The new policy was extended to all of the socialist countries so that in the 1960s Swedish women went to Poland for abortions (Jones 1986).

In this context, social need meant that women could request abortions for nonmedical reasons—a continuation of education, insufficient income, or inadequate housing. These reasons are based on a conception of woman as responsible and not the pathetic victim of rape, incest, or mental disorder. According to the public opinion polls, the same reasons are less acceptable in the United States.

Apart from the ideological differences, the reasons used for requesting an abortion in Eastern Europe reflect a difference in the groups seeking abortion. In Eastern Europe (and in most of Europe) they are typically married women who already have several children; in the United States they tend to be young unmarried women with no previous pregnancies. The former are more present oriented; the latter, more future oriented. Americans find it hard to believe that someone would want an abortion because her apartment was already overcrowded, but do understand why a teenager in school would want one.

The rates of abortion among Eastern European countries, including the Soviet Union, are high, and to some extent can be attributed to lack of experience with contraception. Contraceptives are in short supply and poor in quality. Abortion, then, may function instead of contraception or it may be the result of failed contraception or distrust of the birth-control pill. However, a very careful study carried out in Yugoslavia with matched groups—those who used contraceptives and those who sought abortions—found that the major difference between the two groups is the woman's sense of efficacy (Kapor-Stanulovic and Friedman 1978). The higher her score on efficacy, the more likely she favored and used contraception. The same study found that husbands and wives believe they have the same view about the future, but do not. And each spouse thinks the other agrees with his or her view although the consensus does not exist. When there is genuine choice between abortion and contraception, where neither decision has any judgmental loading against it, there is a gender factor in the decision making and the choices arrived at.

The strong demand for abortion strains the services, so that abortions are often performed on an outpatient basis or in overcrowded hospitals where women receive no preliminary counseling and are given little or no anaesthetic and follow-up nursing. The pressures for speed up are not confined to the socialist world. On the contrary they may be even more common in a private, profit-based clinic (Joffe 1986). Czechoslovakia, according to Heitlinger (1987) is more advanced than the Soviet Union in the techniques used, but the general social and political framework is the same (David and Friedman 1973). In both countries the reasons for a liberal policy are pragmatic, bowing to the inevitability of women who would procure abortions with or without the approval of authorities. Both countries have been impressed as well by studies of unwanted children (children born to women whose request for an abortion was turned down) that show that these children appear to have behavioral and educational problems; in addition, there is evidence of physical abuse.

Abortion, then, is made easier in the socialist countries than elsewhere. The obstacles are bureaucratic and technological rather than social. Moral judgments are not passed on women who seek the services, and there is no reason for women to fear the untrained or undertrained persons who flourish where abortion is illegal or beyond the means of most people. Nevertheless, women are often troubled by the abortion. A study carried out in Hungary and Yugoslavia based on follow-up interviews with women who had abortions found a significant number who just a year later could not remember having had the abortion. They were mainly young and unmarried, and it had been their first pregnancy. This suggests that abortion, like childbirth, is learned behavior, easier the second and third time than the first.

Because a large percentage of doctors in socialist countries are women, the likelihood of having a woman physician carry out the abortion would seem to be fairly good. But in Czechoslovakia the occupational structure is different; women remain the general practitioners, but men have begun to claim the high-status specializations. Only about a third in the obstetrics and gynecology group are women (Heitlinger 1987). Hence, men are more apt to do abortions than women, and this gender difference may explain why the methods used are more technologically sophisticated. (Whether the recently developed steroid treatment RU-486 developed by the Roussel-Uclaf company of France will be available in countries where the pharmaceutical industries are run on a nonprofit basis remains to be seen. It is being kept off the market in the United States by anti-choice pressure groups.)

Until now there has been nothing in the socialist countries comparable to the anti-abortion groups in the United States nor has the women's movement put abortion on its agenda. Recent developments toward greater tolerance of traditional religions may generate an anti-abortion movement, although even in Catholic Poland the politicians who expressed sympathy with the Vatican's views were unwilling to make abortion illegal and contribute, they said, to the incidence of illegal abortions or to the phenomenon familiar to Europeans of women going outside of the country to have abortions. At the same time, the democratization process in Eastern Europe may also mean a reconsideration of abortion as an individual constitutional right.

Conclusion

Considering the three models—preliterate, Victorian, socialist—we can see how persistent abortion is and how its practices are different in different contexts. Not all societies have a biomedical model of pregnancy as a disorder, and only in those which have a nuclear family do we see an image of the fetus as a person.

From a broader perspective, we can see that abortion occurs in different societal contexts. The question, then, is not just pro-choice or family policy, but what kind of a society do we want: one with or without procreative freedom. And if procreation is a choice, on what basis can we, or should we, discriminate between proactive choice (contraception) and reactive choice (abortion).

Finally, the history of procreative choice has been related to certain levels of economic and political development. There is a correlation between underdevelopment and government or state population policy. A similar correlation exists between the industrial-developed economies and birth control controlled by individuals. If economic development in North America occurs at the expense of development in other parts of the world, as many social critics argue, the moral equation changes. Women in North America have procreative choice at the expense of women elsewhere, just as their economic status may be obtained at the expense of other women. An interdependent global economy has linked us all together. In that sense ours is a pseudo-choice. If women in the less developed countries have their choices or the lack of them determined by the government or by imposed policies of population control, there is no genuine choice for them. Indirectly, they are subsidizing the procreative choice of their counterparts in Europe and North America. Just as the economy of production and consumption have become global, the economy of reproduction has become global and inter-dependent.

Chapter 3

Teenage Pregnancy: The Double Standard and the Limitations of Contraception

Pregnancy and the End of Innocence

Adolescence occupies a very special place in American life. The combination of early puberty, an extended educational system, and late entry into the labor force has given this age group more freedom, more time to grow up before taking on adult responsibility. Adolescence is sheltered by a veil of innocence and leisure combined with the hopes and projections of parents. But the illusion is shattered by a reality in which each year one million teenage girls become pregnant and just slightly more than half that number give birth to children. Most are poor, most are unmarried, and most had not intended to become pregnant. They have entered the adult world through a back door, abruptly and unprepared.

Statistically, the birthrate of adolescents in the United States resembles the high birthrates of the third world (Jones et al. 1986). It is a function of poverty and the culture of poverty, just as the low birthrate among middle-class women is a function of an affluent economic and social environment. Again, the two worlds are inter-dependent. But our purpose in studying teenage pregnancy and abortion is not to compare the two worlds or the two socioeconomic classes within our own society, but to illustrate, first, the limitations of contraception and, second, the double standard of sexuality in which the male partner has sexual privileges without responsibility.

97

Why, unlike the socialist bloc countries, where the highest rates of abortion are among women over the age of 26, are the highest rates of abortion in the United States in the 15- to 19-year-old class? Teenage pregnancy and subsequent abortion represent some kind of failure in a modernization scenario that links economic growth, deferred gratification, small and late families. In the past, families were larger and a young mother would have had an early marriage. Together, she and her spouse would have had a network of neighbors and relatives connected in a system of communal support. Children would not have been easily abandoned or seriously neglected. That system still prevails in many closed religious communities and, as well, on an Israeli kibbutz where the age of parents scarcely matters. Children are highly desired; the responsibility of providing their material needs, nurturing, and education is assumed by the kibbutz and shared by their parents and other adults. But in the inner cities of Chicago, New York, and San Francisco, the pregnant 15-year-old is not likely to have an extended kinship system, community support, or a stable relationship with her partner. Glendon (1987) points out that American society is the most permissive among developed societies in terms of abortion and the most underdeveloped in terms of family policy. Until we have a system of social security for children and a comprehensive system of family welfare, the pregnant woman, regardless of class, is sacrificed for the welfare of the newborn. The food will come out of her mouth, not her older children's; the time will come out of her rest, not her husband's; the employment, promotion, and income given up is hers, not his. (There is greater risk of fetal defect in the late pregnancies. With more professional women delaying childbearing and with better prenatal testing, we can expect an increase in abortion in the 30 to 40 age group that may change the shape of the curve.) Almost all of the costs, then, of an additional child will be borne disproportionately by the woman. If she is a young woman and living below the poverty line, her future will probably include dropping out of school. If the pregnancy is carried to term and she decides to keep the child, she will be handicapped in terms of future earning power. Chances are she will be on welfare, repeating the pattern of her mother. Any short-term gains in social learning, in growing-up fast, then, are canceled by the overwhelming loss of whatever hope she might have had of leading a self-sufficient, self-directing, independent life without the opiates of game shows and soap operas.

Some of these statistics could have been avoided by better sex education. Women, especially young women, do not always understand their own bodies and believe or want to believe that a woman cannot get pregnant during her first experience of intercourse. There are also widespread misconceptions about the types of contraceptives available and their proper use. The younger the woman, the less informed, the less developed she is in terms of her own cognitive development, the less able she is to make complex decisions (Resnick 1984). Nevertheless, contraception, which is as much a social technology as a mechanical one, depends on the experience of the person using it. Use of the pill and the IUD (intrauterine device) assumes a stable relationship in which sexual intercourse is a regularized phenomenon. Women of all ages, but inexperienced adolescents more so, run the risk of becoming pregnant when their relationships are casual or uncommitted, without any expectation of continuity.

The Cult and Culture of Masculinity

Some of the statistics could have been avoided, too, by better access to contraceptive services. Public hospitals are typically underfunded and too overused to maintain good 24-hour services for teenagers and their partners. But, more important than sexual ignorance or limited access, is the cultural milieu that equates masculinity with virility. To be sexually active, worldly wise, and superbly competent, to have effortless erections and frequent ejaculations, is the fantasy of the male adolescent and is shared with his friends as part of his self-presentation. Femininity is thus shaped reciprocally by a cultural symbol of the young male stud encouraged to "sow his wild oats" and rewarded by his male peers for "making out" with as many virgins as he can. Pregnancy, far from being seen as a reprimand, becomes proof of his identity as an adult, *macho* and heterosexual. The complementary role is the young woman, as eager to explore her sexuality as he is, who may want to assert her adult independence and identity through sexual performance. A few, consciously or unconsciously, may want a baby to raise on their own; others may want marriage; but most want neither. The more we learn about how and why teenage pregnancy happens, the more evidence we have of asymmetrical gender roles. The decision to use a contraceptive, jointly made, is more often his than hers. Yet he may be overly confident of his ability to withdraw, too ready to take risks without condoms, and unwilling to make the long-term commitment that would be involved in expecting the girl to use an oral contraceptive. His pleasure and his convenience are more important than delay. As long as this inequality prevails, "Just Say No" campaigns are doomed to failure.

The decision to terminate the pregnancy, to deal with the consequences of gender inequality, falls on her shoulders, and her youthful partner may be spared any knowledge of it, any sense of irresponsibility. Ironically, older women, married and middle-aged women, are often reluctant to tell their partners or husbands, even their family doctors, about a suspected pregnancy and contemplated abortion. Fear, embarrassment, and wanting to avoid a quarrel may be some of the reasons, but no less important is the concept of decisional privacy (Allen 1988): "It is my business, no one else's. If I decide to have the baby they will all know about it soon enough." And if abortion is criminal, she has even more reason to keep her thoughts to herself as she plans a strategy of contravening a law she can no longer afford to respect.

Thus, the criminalization of abortion becomes a woman's problem, and her behavior is judged by psychiatrists, doctors, health care workers, and others. In contrast, the male's behavior is not subject to scrutiny although he may receive a slap on the wrist. (There are other systems of informal social control.) In addition, the criminalization of abortion creates its own kind of coercive privacy. When the Supreme Court granted women the right to privacy (*Roe v. Wade*) in the first trimester of a pregnancy, it was only returning what criminalization had earlier taken away.

For the adolescent the problems are many. If she is to have any choice of options, she must act quickly, covertly, and decisively. In a very short time she must process biological, medical, psychological, social, and legal information. If she is sure she is pregnant, she must decide whether to tell her partner, and they may disagree about what should be done. In addition, she must negotiate a series of pressures—a mother who says, "I'll raise the child"; a boyfriend who says, "Get rid of it"; a priest who says, "Give it up for adoption"; an aunt who says, "Whatever you do, don't marry him"; a father who says, "You got yourself into this mess, now get yourself out of it"; a friend who has a friend who has a friend who knows what to do to start periods again; and a clinic counselor who says, "The decision is and must be yours, but if you wait too long I can't help you." If she goes to a Catholic secondary school her network of friends may quickly shrink.

In the decision process she loses her privacy.

Here is one woman's account:

I went into the psychiatrist's office and we talked for about half an hour. He asked me several questions. Have I ever had V.D.? What would my parents think if they knew? How many men have I slept with? Why do I want an abortion? How much money do I have in the bank? How much do I earn monthly? How old is my boyfriend? Will I ever get married? Was I using birth control? Why not? What would I do if I didn't get the abortion? If I had the baby, would I keep it or give it up? Had I ever taken drugs? Did I ever try to commit suicide?[24]

As more states pass laws that require parental notification, and as more hospitals and clinics require parental or spouse notification, the pregnant teenager endures even more invasions of her privacy. The situation is worse in small communities where rumors spread fast. Thus, her behavior and motives are open to inspection despite all assurances of professional confidentiality, whereas her partner need not answer questions about his motivation or in other ways explain his actions. In this environment a do-it-yourself soap and Lysol douche can be a more attractive alternative. Many times these treatments succeed by poisoning the woman, who is lucky to survive. But the process, even when benign, is likely to make her feel she is being punished for being a woman, not for what she did, for what she did could not have been accomplished by herself alone.

Her problems are not over when she chooses abortion. Gaining access to abortion services may involve finding a clinic where parental notification is not required. If she is poor she must find one that is free or affordable. In general, white middle-class teenagers have abortions in private clinics, whereas black, low-income teenagers have theirs in public facilities, a difference that might explain why the abortions of the first group are performed earlier (in the first trimester) and those of the second are often performed later. Public patients experience more complications, especially in the second trimester, than the others (Tietze and Lewit 1973).

The Choice of Abortion

As we noted earlier, not all who choose abortion believe in that choice for others. Teenagers who have thought less about it have their own rationale. The reason most give for wanting an abortion is age: "I think I am too young to have a child." And when they elaborate, it becomes clear that they have a strong sense of responsibility about child rearing. One of many examples is the 15-year-old who said:

> Mom got married when she was 16; she had me when she was 17, and she got divorced when she was 18. Now that's not the ideal in life, and I don't want it to be the same way.[25]

Women who are more mature are also age-conscious. In their case, they feel too old for the responsibility. But they are spared the stereotype of the teenage woman as impulse-driven, sexual tease who prefers welfare to school or work and made the mistake of getting "caught." The parallel, however, is between the teenage woman saying she is too young and the older woman saying, "My family is complete. I've paid my dues."

The American Psychological Association conducted a review of the psychological and legal issues of adolescent abortion and concluded that there were no special problems that applied to adolescents that did not apply to adult women as well (Melton 1986). There was no need for legislation that was based on the young-age group. The major psychological reaction to abortion was relief; more complex feelings tapered off quickly (Adler and Dolcini 1986). Indeed, despite anecdotal data, if the young woman had no previous history of psychiatric problems, there were no short- or long-term psychological reactions that would require any special therapeutic intervention. The earlier the abortion, the fewer postabortion problems; the stronger the support system the woman had— her male partner, her parents, the physician (Greenglass 1976)—the less difficult were her problems. Women identified with religious denominations strongly opposed to abortion experienced more conflict. But when the group that had abortions was matched and compared with a group who carried their pregnancies to term with plans to put the babies up for adoption, the group that had abortions had fewer negative reactions or psychological difficulties.

On the other side are the pro-life psychologists who interpret these data differently. If the woman committing a wrong feels no guilt, there is, indeed, something wrong in her psychological state. The "absence of postabortion guilt feelings," Ganz writes, "would be a clear indication that abortion (aside from being morally wrong) is extremely dangerous to a woman's psychological health because it dulls her moral sensitivity and deadens her conscience."[26]

Counseling and the Value Systems of Counselors

Without trying to resolve these gender, race, and class inequities, many people feel that teenage abortion is unique, a lag somewhere in the evolution of American society, and that because it is more the adults' failure than the teenagers' the scales should be tipped in favor of abortion as a free choice.

Toughness as a Deterrent

According to some scholars, easy access to abortion will only make worse what is already a pandemic problem. More teenagers will become more promiscuous and, as a result, pregnant. If this becomes a norm, it will become a habit. More abortions will be sought, and the same people will have multiple abortions. Being tough, then, is being kind and in the best interest of minors. Further, it offers some positive reinforcement to the marginal teenagers who need some official legitimation for their resistance to unprotected sex. This reasoning is similar to the fear that legalizing drugs will increase the population of addicts, whereas making drugs illegal will help those who feel pulled in both directions.

The punishment for the pregnant teenager has taken a peculiar form. Shame and ostracism are combined with allowing the young woman to have an abortion on condition that there is parental consent. Most teenagers do discuss abortion with at least one of their parents, and those who do not usually have good reasons for not doing so. There may be a deep estrangement between them or a history of family violence. The father or stepfather may even be responsible for the pregnancy. In such cases, the court may allow the girl to appeal directly to the judge. But the entire process is so intimidating and humiliating that a 17-year old who has never been inside a courtroom or talked directly to a judge and who is unfamiliar with her rights becomes desperate and looks for other ways of terminating the pregnancy (Bonavoglia 1990). Whether this teaches her to be careful in the future is doubtful because she thought she was being careful this time.

Learning as a Deterrent

A better method of deterrence, according to some, is to give the pregnant young person the benefit of the doubt and a second chance. At the very least, this approach accepts the reality of sexual activity and emphasizes contraception. Tomas Silber, a pediatrician and bioethicist, has proposed that abortion is justified, but that the abortion and abortion counseling should become a learning experience. Just once, and only once.

> I do see the imperative for the adolescent girl not to repeat her mistake. The sacrifice of the fetus should be followed by a compromise (abstinence, contraception, responsible sex, family planning). From this viewpoint, a

second abortion should be considered unethical when it implies betrayal of the assumed compromise.[27]

Silber does not rule out a second abortion, but, he says, it has lost any claim to ethical status and the woman forfeits our willingness to waive the rules that apply to others; a contract has been broken. Women sometimes express a similar judgment: One abortion is a privilege, two is an abuse. "I don't think you should continuously kill them off like that. If you don't want them just get sterilized. If you can't get sterilized or use birth control, get used to little feet running around the house."[28]

The same conditional approval is found in Joffe (1966) who describes her own experience working in a clinic. Clinic counselors go to great lengths to help a youngster through an abortion. Despite the emotional stress of the work, they are, as they say, "there for her" from the decision-making stage through the postpartum depression at the end. But if the same 15-year-old becomes a repeater and returns at 16 and at 17, and if she develops a cool attitude toward the counseling experience, the reaction is different. The counselor loses her own professional distance, Joffe says. "The legalization and consequent routinization of abortion has stimulated in the former (the counselor) new questions about the morality of abortion. For the latter (the client), this very same routinization seems to have had the opposite effect."[29]

Too little guilt is as undesirable, then, as too much; the former is a moral issue, the latter a mental health issue. Abortion is no longer a choice. It is, instead, a suspended sentence followed by a period of probation during which a young woman is expected to turn off her sexuality, show better judgment in men, and in general change the patriarchal system that limits any bargaining power she has in the backseat of a car. If she disregards this advice and returns to the clinic she must, at least, appear contrite. Harrison, who makes a very powerful case for pro-choice, is similarly uncomfortable with the unrepentant repeater as if this were a form of recidivism. The repeater also turns up in psychiatric literature as the RA (repeated abortions) syndrome (Honig, Dorshave, Zakut, and Serr 1975). Some are better candidates for psychotherapy than others.

What could be more American or middle-class than believing that an ounce of prevention is worth a pound of cure? But what these examples illustrate is the further oppression of a woman by the lack of an abortion ethic. Pro-choice means that women are free to choose abortion over carrying a baby to term, and free to choose abortion over contraception.

Adoption

Not all social workers believe that individual, one-on-one counseling is appropriate. Family-based counseling starts from the assumption that a pregnancy is not a personal or a private matter, but a family one (Ooms 1984). It has consequences for husbands and other children, for siblings, and for parents and grandparents on both sides. Nor does the circle end with immediate family members. Possible adoptive parents have a stake in the future of the pregnancy, and they, too, should be included although not necessarily physically present. Unless all of these connected people are heard, the pregnant woman is unable to make a truly informed decision. Thus, the pregnant woman, regardless of age, is forced to confront fully the alternatives such as carrying a child to term and giving it up for adoption or keeping it. Abortion is a choice, but, given this extended-obligation model of counseling, it is easy to see how adoption would meet with greater approval. These are the very social workers who keep in touch with physicians who are the first to discover the pregnancy and who may hold the same views as the social worker on adoption. The childless couple shops from doctors to social workers to friends of friends, and the couple's plight is part of the climate of opinion that makes any resistance to adoption that much harder emotionally for the pregnant girl or woman.

Adoption is also the goal of pastoral counseling, but the discourse is moral rather than therapeutic. The strains on the counselor (almost always male) are different, especially for the Catholic counselor who must explore all alternatives, save one: abortion (Häring 1970). "[We] must recognize," Häring (1970) writes, "that although the fetus is innocent, the girl is likewise innocent."[30] The hard cases are difficult and the counselor must help the client to understand why abortion is not morally acceptable. Protestant clergy have more flexibility, but the moral journey with the client can be painful for both (Gustafson 1970). As the counselors formulate the problem, the intellectual challenge is to find a course between formal authority and individual subjectivity, between moral law and "do what feels right to you." Neither Protestant nor Catholic, however, approaches the alternatives in terms of social consequences; it is, as Gustafson puts it, "the primacy of the judgmental posture." Thus the pregnant woman considering abortion and wanting approval is counseled to recognize the ego-centeredness of her reasons and to shift her focus from pragmatic considerations to moral ones. The harshness of this for her must be understood by a sympathetic counselor, but the function of the counselor is to help the woman understand the sanctity of life as given by

God and accept her duty. To disobey this is to condemn oneself to a life of guilt. If there is no sense of guilt associated with abortions, our civilization is demoralized.

The statistics suggest that many Catholic women disregard the church's teaching on abortion and its counseling without rejecting Catholicism as a religious faith. But both the religious and the secular social-work counseling models flounder because they substitute a counseling ethic for a pro-choice ethic.

Finally, there is another type of counseling based on the assumption that preabortion stress is better than postabortion stress (Francke 1978). A deliberate effort is made to create anxiety in the hope that women will have no regrets about having made the wrong decision (to terminate a pregnancy) later; it is "stressful rather than supportive counseling" but sounds like something very close to sadistic counseling.

Conclusion

To summarize, the pressures and privileges of adolescence have given today's young people more opportunity than earlier generations to find their own identity, to experiment and postpone life-long decisions. Sexual exploration has been part of the experience for all socioeconomic groups, and teenage pregnancy has been one of the consequences. It is a problem, however, for adults who project their own ambivalences about sexuality, hedonism, and leisure onto the screen of adolescents. We vacillate between indulgence and punishment; we want to spare them but envy them. It would be interesting to know how teenage women would make their own reproductive decisions if adults were kept out of the picture until their help was needed. Meanwhile, teenagers have become the target group in the abortion backlash as states and other jurisdictions enact regulations that punish young women by requiring them to get parental consent or by withholding abortions if they are unable to pay.

Economically, teenage pregnancy is a problem for low-income groups who do not have the back-up resources for handling the unwanted, unexpected, and unplanned child. Our national concerns about poverty and "children raising children" are part of the larger context. And because we do not have the kinship systems of preliterate societies, or the collective institutions of the Israeli kibbutz, or a social security system for children, we have a social problem. The growth of the problem is cause for concern by both pro-choice and pro-life proponents although they arrive at different analyses of the problem and different proposals for social policy. Rightly or wrongly, we do not accept teenage pregnancy as a norm and are not willing to pay the social costs associated with it. But are we objecting to teenage pregnancy as an age phenomenon? Or to the poverty, racism, and social disorganization that may make pregnancy a rational choice and a compensation? Or to the lack of a decent social infrastructure?

Teenage pregnancy may also serve as a more general model of the unwanted pregnancy. It provides a clear picture of the gender inequality that we all experience in a variety of social situations. The teenage woman who must take responsibility for the consequences of a decision her partner made is a metaphor for other situations of gender dominance and subordination. If the option is abortion and abortion is illegal, the law is also discriminatory, for it is she who can be charged, not her partner. And that, too, can be generalized to other examples of family law.

The counseling process is judgmental even when it is not moralistic. Pastoral counseling is both. Family counseling is more empirical and value-free, but it assumes that abortion would have the same consequences for a family as would having a child. They are not equivalent in theory or practice. Moreover, the original decision to have a child would not ordinarily be discussed with a social worker and with all the parties present. It is difficult, therefore, to understand why abortion should be of greater concern to family and friends. The truth is that family counseling, like pastoral counseling, is based on maintaining the family as a system. If a young, unmarried woman feels unable to keep the child herself, it seems logical to point out to her—as if she didn't know—that there are childless couples whose lives would be enriched by having her child. The focus shifts from the needs of the woman with an unwanted pregnancy to the needs of a childless couple, from abortion to adoption. Social workers who mistakenly believe they can represent both are biased, usually in favor of adoption with its happy familial ending.

Finally, we looked at counseling models where the pregnant client was at the center, the family-planning model in which abortion is not pre-judged but also is not approved if it becomes a frequent habit. Thus, we have a quasi-contractual agreement between two parties, counselor and client. If the abortion experience is not a learning experience, if one party, the client, breaks the contract, the moral deal is canceled and the client is rejected, written off as uneducable. Psychiatry and mental health propose a less contractual model of psychopathology. A repeater is presumed to have some serious problems that require intensive therapy rather than mere abortion counseling. Closely related is the stress counseling that is anti-abortion but not pro-adoption, and has, more than any other form of counseling, some serious ethical problems of mental abuse.

Comparing this situation with the one in Eastern Europe where abortion is an accepted part of family planning and women typically have several abortions during their child-bearing years without anyone probing their psyches, the latter looks infinitely more enlightened. When the two situations are juxtaposed, it becomes apparent that it is the counselor who needs the counseling. The client who is more realistic knows that contraception is not fail-safe, that sexual power is still a male prerogative, and that there is nothing deviant about preferring abortion to contraception.

A fourth type of counseling that we have not dealt with here is the medical counseling that serves as the gateway to adoption and a therapeutic abortion. For that, however, we need to look more closely at the biomedical models of abortion.

Chapter 4

Three Patterns of Discourse

The Medical Model and Therapeutic Abortion

Abortion: Biological or Social?

The compromise between no abortion and elective abortion is the therapeutic abortion, an abortion that requires the approval of a physician who has to certify that continuing a pregnancy would be detrimental to the physical or mental health of the woman or that there is evidence of gross fetal deformity. For pro-choice groups, it is the worst of both worlds; abortion is criminal and women are required to find a sympathetic physician and persuade this person that some current or past history of a physical or mental incapacity is serious enough to warrant a therapeutic abortion. Social reasons are not acceptable, and the woman's own judgment is not considered sufficient. It is, indeed, the privileged therapeutic abortion that was challenged by the *Roe v. Wade* decision of 1973 and that went part of the way toward making elective abortion a right.

Pro-life groups who were opposed to abortion in principle found therapeutic abortion just as abhorrent. Their fears that therapeutic abortions would be used broadly, if not indiscriminately, were to some extent justified. Different hospitals, for example, had different rates of therapeutic abortions (Frame 1978). In many jurisdictions physicians measured the mother's health against the yardstick of the World Health Organization's definition of health; that is, being well meant well-being. This, then, was the nightmare of what has come to be called the *slippery slope*.

Most women were neither pro- nor anti-choice. In the course of time they adapted to the new legal environment and learned to use it expediently, but not without some sense of alienation. Their collective voice was heard in public opinion polls and was eventually recognized by the U.S. Supreme Court's discussion of abortion as "privacy." The concept of "decisional privacy" (Allen 1988) expresses perfectly the intuitive sense of American women that decisions on reproduction are personal and private, neither medical nor part of larger systems of ideology. Meanwhile, and before the landmark decisions on privacy and abortion, illegal abortions continued among the less-educated and the poor, and so did maternal mortality.

Therapeutic abortion is based on a biomedical model of pregnancy that recognizes two, and only two, types of abortion: spontaneous and therapeutic. All others are either illegal or do not require the knowledge and understanding of a physician. The first, the spontaneous abortion, occurs when some unforeseen idiosyncratic factor interrupts the gestation process and results in a miscarriage or stillbirth. Thus, the pregnancy is terminated, sometimes with the assistance of a physician, and the woman's normal cycles of ovulation resume. The woman, however exemplary her habits and lifestyle, has very little influence on the probability of having a spontaneous abortion. One woman who takes good care of herself may have several miscarriages; another who is overly active, sleeps too little, and eats a diet of junk food may carry a fetus to term without once spotting or having any cause to doubt the successful outcome. A spontaneous abortion is, as the saying goes, nature's way of dealing with its own errors.

What is missing from this model is an awareness that the pregnancy process is as much social and cultural as biological. If, for example, the rates of spontaneous abortion are low, it is because women choose to have children in the low-risk years of their life cycle. If the rates are high, it may be because more women are simulating spontaneous abortions for various reasons. For example, when abortion was prohibited in the 19th century, the rate of miscarriages and stillbirths increased despite improving obstetrical care. Dr. Andrew Nebinger, who brought these statistics to the attention of the Philadelphia County Medical Society in 1870, was probably correct in his inference. These statistics, he said:

indicate a mortality . . . too great to be attributed to the ordinary accidental or unavoidable causes which are generally operative in the production of stillbirth. . . . therefore, it is fair to attribute the great excess to avoidable causes; or, in other words, the result of criminal intentions and acts on the part of the mother and her abettors.[31]

But the major criticism of the biomedical model has come from scientists working with a more holistic and interactive conception of the body. The older mind–body dualism and the nature–nurture dichotomies have been challenged by stress-related disorders, psychosomatic medicine, and ecology. Thus, a spontaneous abortion may be an unexpected surprise for the pregnant woman, but endemic in her community (e.g., Love Canal) or her social class or some other group characteristic. Public policy on abortion has gradually begun to recognize the new understanding of fertility, infertility, and fetal loss. Greater attention is given to social and environmental causality. Consider famine. It is surely one of the cruelties of nature that a woman can become pregnant under famine conditions that deprive her of the nutrients for sustaining a pregnancy. Other kinds of environmental factors—water pollution, low-level radiation, toxic wastes—can also produce fetal defects and fetal wastage. In addition, there are prescription drugs or diseases like rubella that have as one of their side effects the disruption of fetal development. Sexual assault and emotional trauma, especially including political events, can be life-threatening to fetal development. And finally, there is the abortion sought either because sex education on contraception was inadequate or because contraception itself was unavailable, inefficient, or produced iatrogenic effects. One example, a woman in her thirties and a university graduate, will suffice:

I have conscientiously practised birth control and have subjected myself, over the past ten years, to such unpleasant and perhaps dangerous methods as the pill, two different IUDs, foam and finally a diaphragm and jelly (which I was using when I became pregnant). When on the pill I tried several different brands and they all produced in me a bloated uncomfortable body, mood swings, depression, and a general feeling of not being myself. I persevered for several years. . . . I doubt if that many men would be prepared to subject their bodies to that kind of abuse."[32]

There are, then, three types of spontaneous abortion: the aberrant pregnancy, the simulated one, and the one that is the consequence of exogenous factors. It is misleading to call all of them spontaneous. They are in varying degrees involuntary and reflect a more social model of pregnancy and abortion.

The second type of abortion, the therapeutic abortion, makes many of the same assumptions about pregnancy—that it responds to inner signals including the ticking of the biological clock; that it follows a sequence of development that a woman cannot alter; and that, in short, the body answers to itself. Nevertheless, a woman whose health is frail may not be able to handle the pregnancy if she is under acute emotional distress—what Williams (1970) calls a social and psychological ectopic pregnancy. There may be sound reasons for terminating a pregnancy, preferably early, but these reasons do not necessarily result in an abortion. Even though the principle of ectopic pregnancies is well established, physicians who understand may be reluctant to offer an opinion and insist that the woman see a psychiatrist; they may refuse to carry out the procedure and refer her to someone else.

More controversial are cases where a woman is in good health but has learned from fetal testing that there is evidence of serious fetal abnormality. Modern developments in fetal imaging have made it possible to detect large classes of fetal disorders early in a pregnancy. Women who delay childbearing until their late thirties (often professional women; often second marriages) are advised to undergo amniocentesis, chorionic villi biopsies, and other diagnostic screening tests. Although the tests are not perfect—there are false positives and false negatives—they are reliable enough either to reassure a woman or to warn her of the probability of a tragic outcome: a brain damaged child, an infant who can only survive for a few days, a child who would require full-time care throughout its life, children so deformed they can have no hope of developing normally.

Balancing this are the miracles of fetal surgery that can, in some cases, intervene and correct the defects. The career needs and enthusiasm of these surgeons may put considerable pressure on the woman to, at least, try: "You owe it to your baby to give it a chance, but we're warning you that the results could be worse." Good medical ethics would separate the two groups of specialists, obstetricians from fetal surgeons, and, in any case, they may disagree among themselves.

Pro-life supporters have seized upon these examples of fetal surgery to say that no fetus need be aborted. The fallacy here is not to recognize that medical knowledge can only provide medical information; there is no expertise beyond that. Physicians often acknowledge their limitations and accept the fact that pregnancy and abortion are only partially medical events. If they are prudent, they also acknowledge there may be conflicting medical opinions. Nothing, in fact, has been changed by the new high-technologies except that informed consent becomes more difficult. The woman's options are the same, to terminate a pregnancy or not. Medical caregivers can be of limited help, for they lack all the parts in the larger matrix of decision making. The obstetrician or the surgeon has no way of knowing the trauma of fetal surgery for the woman. Only she can answer that, and legally she has the right to refuse treatment.

One Pregnancy, Two Patients

Medical students are routinely taught that from the time a conception has been verified they have two patients and that unless some crisis develops forcing them to choose they have an equal obligation to both (Stotland 1988). This kind of thinking contributes to the bonding between woman and fetus that is matched by the physiological dependence of the fetus on the woman. Calling the fetus a patient also helps to humanize it. Pro-life and right-to-life supporters take this to mean that the fetus is a form of human life and that, therefore, terminating it would be tantamount to killing a patient. Dr. Bernard Nathanson writes

> I have spent my life in the practice of obstetrics and gynaecology and have watched as the attention of the specialty has turned from a preoccupation with the maternal welfare to the welfare of the unborn child. It is the transcendant irony in the history of medicine that as increasing scientific attention and enormous resources were being assigned by the medical community to the protection and welfare of the unborn child, a new liberty was being quarried out of the United States Constitution which permitted and even encouraged the mass scale destruction of the child."[33]

But is patienthood the same as personhood? Ruddick (1988) argues they are not the same. Patienthood entitles the fetus to care and to be spared indignities, but it does not automatically entitle it to life. Psychologically, patient one's attitude may change toward patient two as the pregnancy advances. Their dependencies may be reversed as the woman becomes more attached emotionally to the fetus. But the fact that a woman and her physician may view the fetus differently in the first trimester from the way they view it in the second or third is irrelevant to the abortion question.

One Patient, One Enemy

Ruddick's sequential model assumes a shifting pattern in the relationship between pregnant woman and fetus culminating in a mother and child relationship. However, in another class of cases the future mother becomes the present enemy of the fetus, not because she chooses abortion, as pro-life supporters would claim, but because her life-style endangers the fetus.

In the 19th century, the birth of a child with some form of fetal defect was attributed to heredity or some problem with the male's sperm. Toward the end of the 19th century more attention was given to the transmission of syphilis and gonorrhea to the infant. Contemporary science has shifted the focus to women whose life-styles are threatening to normal fetal development.

What lies behind this trend is a new understanding of the placenta which, in the past, was regarded as a good barrier to any kind of exogenous and noxious influence. That complacency has been reconsidered, for it now appears that the placenta is not impermeable. Thus, a woman who consumes large quantities of alcohol runs the risk of giving birth to an infant with fetal alcohol syndrome. Other substances, such as hard drugs like cocaine, heroin, and "crack," are similarly deleterious. Although these substances have been the most publicized, the more common across-the-counter medications may be problematic as well: aspirin, nose drops, laxatives, and all forms of relaxants or stimulants such as caffeine and tobacco, not to mention tranquilizers. Judging from the popular manuals for gravid women, a modern pregnancy has become an exercise in asceticism.

Considerable controversy surrounds these new behavioral patterns in a neonate. Exactly what constitutes the syndrome—low birthweight? mental retardation? erratic sleep patterns? Can good neonatal care reverse the effects? Despite the controversy, however, there is now wide acceptance that the health and survival of the fetus is related to the behavior of women during the pregnancy (McCormack, 1990). It is on this basis that a physician may feel he or she has but one patient, the fetus. The other patient, an addicted woman, is dangerous and must be managed if the physician is not to lose his patient. Management may mean being compelled to enter a detox clinic and remain under surveillance for the duration of the pregnancy. Going one step further, women who disregard warnings about the use of noxious substances can be, and have been, accused of child abuse. Family court judges have seen this disregard as justification for removing newborn infants from a woman whom they regard as an unfit mother and placing the newborn in foster homes. It is the scenario, par excellence, of fetal rights versus maternal rights in which the rights of the fetus are derived from the metaphor of the fetus as patient. Maternal rights become contingent on whether the woman is or is not an unfit mother.

Summary

To summarize, much of our thinking and law on abortion are based on the biological model of reproduction and the medicalization of pregnancy. But, as we have seen, the biological–medical component is a diagnostic and treatment one; other components are social. Thus, abortions are neither spontaneous nor anticipated; they are more or less involuntary. The therapeutic abortion stands on its own, neither elective nor spontaneous. In theory, the therapeutic abortion was intended to protect the woman who, for physical or psychological reasons, could not carry the fetus to term. A different type of therapeutic abortion may take place that is contingent on the welfare of the fetus. At any time during a pregnancy, a woman may learn from tests that the fetus is in serious trouble and that without surgical intervention its survival may be in jeopardy. Whether the medical team changes position with the obstetrician allowing the pediatrician to step ahead may depend on whether the pregnancy is in the first, second, or third trimester. But in cases where the woman's life-style disregards the health of the fetus, the physician's patient is the fetus, who must be protected from the woman carrying it.

The therapeutic abortion is a form of control that reinforces the role of medical professionals—obstetricians, fetal surgeons, anesthetists, and others in the health care system. Inevitably, the trend is toward defining pregnancies as high risk and toward high-tech abortions that require hospitalization and the services of a team. Low-tech abortions that can be conducted safely in a clinic and call for a trained assistant plus cookies and juice are discouraged. Medical professionals, then, have a vested interest in the therapeutic abortion.

But the medicalization of pregnancy and abortion also conceals the degree to which others, the woman in particular, determine the final decision. Like any other decision, this one is negotiated; but the woman's role is reactive, selecting among alternatives placed before her by others who share the same medical ideology. The therapeutic abortion controlled by the medical establishment may be preferable to a system of control by the church or the state, particularly the latter, which has wide powers, but it perpetuates the dependency of women. It is pro-abortion, within limits, but not pro-choice.

The implication of our analysis of the therapeutic abortion is this: The category of therapeutic abortion can be eliminated, and all abortions, except those that are involuntary—spontaneous, simulated, or environmentally induced—can be classified as elective. This relocates final authority from the medical establishment to the gravid woman and those whom she chooses to advise her. Elective abortion, however, does not necessarily demedicalize pregnancy or abortion. Women will continue to seek medical advice and to make sense, however best they can, of the information available. Improved methods of fetal surgery may provide an opportunity she will or will not wish to take, but, because the abortion is elective, not therapeutic, she can resist the coercion of high-tech fetal surgeons to let them try. In the moral perspective that we examine next, these empirical questions are regarded as symptomatic of a secular mind-set that has become insensitive to the moral issues.

The Moral Model and the Problem of Fetal Life

What is a fetus? What is a mother? Medical science provides one concept of a fetus; religion and philosophy, another. In one case, the fetus is a patient whose physical health is being monitored; in the other, it is a soul whose spiritual health is at stake. Medical elites are replaced by moral elites, whereas scientific embryology gives way to Christian embryology. They are two distinct forms of discourse, one based on "is," the other on "ought."

Public opinion polls, frequency statistics on abortion, and studies of cross-cultural differences are no longer relevant. They may be important for laws and public policy, but they shed no light on the morality of abortion. Clearing them away, however, does not make the task easier. Within the moral framework exist different theological and philosophical traditions with respect to abortion—whether it is ever justified, whether it is justified under certain circumstances, whether it is always justified. These questions may be linked to contraception, to infanticide, or to other aspects of reproduction. Scholars do not always arrive at the same conclusions.

At one end of the spectrum is the absolute categorical prohibition of abortion that equates it with the crime of homicide. "To kill a normal child sleeping in his crib," Schwarz (1990) writes, "is a terrible evil. Killing a child in an incubator . . . is no less evil. Abortion is killing a child in the incubator of his mother's womb."[34] No exceptions can be made. "The unborn child," Frame (1978) writes, "must not be put to death for the sin of a parent."[35]

At the other extreme is a moral defense of compulsory abortion (Williams 1970). Among Catholic theologians, there are differences between liberals and conservatives (Doncel 1984), whereas liberation theologies, the new religious historians, and feminist spirituality movements have broadened the scope of religious history and the interpretation of the texts. More tolerant of sexuality and less misogynist, the new religious historians have made the case for pro-choice without surrendering a religious commitment or cutting themselves off from a religious community.

Only other religious scholars can judge how successful the new historians and spirituality movements have been, but their efforts have demonstrated, first, that the Christian tradition is not, and has never been, consistent. Its views on abortion have varied depending on how procreative sex was valued and, indeed, on procreation itself. Second, abortion was of no great interest until the late 19th century; until then theological minds were preoccupied with adultery, contraception, celibacy. In general, there was more silence than declaration. "What is surprising to the critical observer," Harrison writes, "is that abortion received so little treatment among Christians or in certain geographical areas or epochs of the church."[36] And finally, the specific argument that the termination of a pregnancy is the killing of an innocent life is even more recent, for although we can find precedents that prohibited abortion, they were widely disregarded by lay as well as religious leaders.

Theological and philosophical discussions of abortion are highly abstract and decontextualized. There is almost no awareness that the moral decision made by a pregnant woman carrying an unwanted pregnancy is specific to that pregnancy; her coordinates are the here and now. Take the case of a woman with a religious background who is asking a religious question that theologians have declined to answer. Her question is not what is a fetus, but what is a mother; not when does a fetus become human, but when does a woman become a mother:

> I was wondering the other day how God would feel about having an abortion. But I don't think people should bring a child into the world that they can't provide for or give them the things they need.[37]

The moral and theological discussions of abortion in this woman's mind are not taken seriously because her right to ask them is not legitimated. Theological disputations on abortion are intended to preempt the moral reasoning of the woman just cited by providing answers to moral questions rather than by providing a moral methodology.

For our purposes, then, we want to look first at the mainstream Christian tradition.

Life or Person?

The crux of the debate is the status of the fetus. According to Christian thought, the fetus possesses a soul that it acquires in and during the gestation process of the gravid woman. Terms like *soul* and *ensoulment* sound strange to our secular ears, as unnatural as some of the belief systems of preliterate societies. But if these terms are not taken literally, they denote a status that is something more than a biological entity with material needs and interests; something less than saintliness. The closest one can come to understanding ensoulment is to think of it as spirituality, a quality which, at the low end of the scale, differentiates us from plants and animals and, at the high end of the scale, motivates us to undertake heroic acts of martyrdom.

Throughout the literature on abortion, three questions are posed: Is the fetus human? When does it become human? And does this status make abortion an act of homicide? The answers to these questions determine whether abortion may be justified. Most of the discussion concerns the second question, when does the fetus become human. There is a practical reason for that because abortion before ensoulment breaks no divine law. Yet this question seems peculiar for our intuitive understanding of morality. Why would the church be more interested in *when* than *why?* Revisionists have turned more to the *why* question, but the mainstream Catholic and Protestant theologies are overwhelmingly concerned with finding the line between subhuman and human, between a period when abortion might be justified in the eyes of God and the period when it is a clear violation of divine law.

One test used was quickening, a state of fetal development that women themselves recognized. Quickening, however, was only indirect proof of a soul and not a reliable one. An active fetus or one that becomes active early shortens the period when a woman could have an abortion with impunity. Viability, the ability to survive outside of the womb, has been another measure used; but it, too, depends too much on circumstances, for example the resources available to care for a premature infant. Weight in grams has sometimes been used. But theologians have wanted an earlier and more objective criterion.

Pope John Paul II shares the position of many traditional thinkers in saying that the conceptus becomes human shortly after the implantation of the fertilized ovum in the uterus. "The unborn child," Frame writes, "belongs (in the most ultimate sense) not to his parents, or to human society in general, or to government, but to God."[38] Our lives begin in God, writes Ramsey (1968):

The value of a human life is ultimately grounded in the value God is placing on it. Anyone can himself stand imaginatively even for a moment within an outlook where everything is referred finally to God—who, from things that are not, brings into being the things that are—should be able to see that God's deliberations about the man need have only begun. If there is anything incredible here, it is not the science, but the pitch of faith which no science proves, disproves or confirms.[39]

In an effort to combine Christian embryology and scientific embryology, Noonan (1984) and others emphasize the genetic code. According to Noonan,

> The positive argument for conception as the decisive moment of humanization is that at conception the new being receives the genetic code. It is this genetic information which determines his characteristics, which is the biological carrier of the possibility of human wisdom, which makes him a self-evolving being. A being with a human genetic code is man.[40]

Not all scientists share his view, and, indeed, few are willing to speculate whether the genetic code means anything more than a set of predispositions. Scientific concepts are heuristic, and when they are less useful as explanatory principles, they are forgotten. Today's embryology based on the genetic code may be replaced at some future time. Noonan's interest in the genetic code opens up the field of genetic engineering for philosophers to explore, but it does not settle the question of abortion.

What is a genetic code? It means something very specific to scientists, but for lay people it translates as a unique hereditary legacy, a set of predispositions of which no two are alike. Predictions about future behavior based on a knowledge of the genetic code are no more exact or reliable than such predictions have been in the past. All that modern science can tell us is that the zygote-embryo-fetus that eventually becomes a neonate brings a set of tendencies or capacities. But these tendencies remain dormant or deteriorate if they are not developed after birth in and through human relations. We come into the world with a capacity for speech but do not develop it without the interaction of others. Similarly, we come into the world with a capacity for parenting, but whether we become a biological parent or an adoptive one, our capacities are all indeterminate and depend on how the social world has structured the family. Studies of infants who have been isolated for long periods demonstrate that physical, social, and mental development are irreversibly arrested. Solitary confinement typically induces a form of dehumanization in social interaction. Thus, like the heart and lungs, the genetic code is a condition for development but does not, as the heart and lungs do not, make us human. They make us, as one writer (Engelhardt 1983) puts it, a member of the species, but "what is of prime moral interest is not species membership, but whether an entity is in fact a person."[41]

Potential and Potentiality as Process

A distinction is sometimes made between person and potential person. The zygote-embryo-fetus is not a fully formed person but has the capacity for becoming one, and that, in itself, gives it a special human status. By terminating a pregnancy, one is killing something that has the potential of becoming a person in the future. The same argument, of course, would be true of contraception.

Potentiality is a particularly attractive idea for a future-oriented culture like ours. Proud parents look into the crib of a newborn infant and see a Nobel Prize winner, a chief justice of the Supreme Court, a sports celebrity, an astronaut, a Jane Austen or Tolstoy, Einstein, Florence Nightingale, the CEO of a major corporation. No doubt these fantasies start even earlier, as parents pick our appropriate names, but it is absurd to think that parents do not distinguish between their wish-fulfillment fantasies and reality, between social potentiality and a biological potentiality that creates backaches, nausea, insomnia, and edema. Feinberg (1978) makes the point that present treatment is not related to a future condition. There is no reason, he says, "to demand that someone who will one day be a person *must* be treated as one now."[42]

Closely related to the potentiality argument is the argument based on the stages of development. According to this view, as gestation proceeds, the zygote becomes an embryo, and the embryo becomes a fetus; in each phase the fetus becomes more human, more like a person, and thus the line between being unborn and born, between being a term fetus and a neonate, is scarcely visible. Indeed, a newborn baby is human in the eyes of its parents, but seen otherwise, it is scarcely different from other primates.

The fallacy here is not to realize that what happens as the fetus moves down the birth canal is the transformation of woman to parent; with birth, the imaging and play-acting are ended. When a baby is born its voice is heard, and within hours of being born there is a necessity to communicate. Parents, siblings, grandparents, nurses, and physicians all must read the signs of the infant's pleasures and pains, hunger and satiation, play and fatigue. Through their behavior and through their eyes, the neonate begins to think symbolically. Life truly begins, then, in the bedroom, shed, cabin, tent, igloo, or hospital delivery room, not in the womb.

The dilemma of the Church, according to Doncel (1984), is that it cannot prove that life begins at some point in the gestation process, but it cannot prove that it does not. Thus, according to Doncel, who describes himself as a liberal Catholic, it plays it safe by declaring simply that the fetus is human by definition. The moral question, then, has been answered dogmatically. The woman contemplating an abortion can either agree or disagree, but she is denied the need to sort out the ethical alternatives, to distinguish between two rights or two wrongs, between something right in the short run and wrong in the long run. It is when we are denied the status for making decisions that decisions about abortion (and most other things, as well) may become frivolous. Thus, the Church is responsible for what it most fears. It robs women of moral accountability and leaves them again in a state of dependency.

On the third question—is abortion homicide?—Devine (1984) argues that the fetus has a moral claim on us, that it is special and unique, but that it cannot be murdered any more than it can commit suicide.

It is, then, a matter of faith whether we choose to regard the fetus as human. Pro-choice supporters are similarly guided by faith, but they regard the discussions of ensoulment as fetishizing the fetus. Pro-choice starts from a different question: When does a woman become a mother? It is at that point that she, on her own, excludes the possibility of abortion, when it takes on the meaning of infanticide. But religious doctrine is so obsessed with the fetus that the pregnancy process is only half understood.

Ethics of the Wanted Child

The pro-choice model rests not on the concept of a fetus, but on the concept of a wanted child. Hence, the starting point is the *relationship* between adults and neonates, on personhood as distinct from either fetal life or ensoulment. A rejected child is a child at risk, although the outcome need not be catastrophic—some children flourish on benign neglect and some suffer from overprotection. However, enough is known about the social and psychological histories of unwanted children to suggest that what the Church objects to about abortion can be applied to child rejection; it symbolically destroys life. A wanted child is not an exploited child or one smothered by sentiment, but a child secure in the knowledge of trust and empathy, guided toward realizing its individual potentialities, its ability to find gratification in social relationships.

The concept of a wanted child is a modern one. Throughout most of history, children were needed to contribute to the economy, provide old-age insurance, or build dynasties (Zelizer 1985). They were uneducated, undereducated, trained as royal scions, bought and sold as slaves, forced to work in deep underground mines, and married off to families for opportunistic reasons. Conversely, children could be a liability, another mouth to feed in an economy of scarcity. It is only in our era, in modern industrial economies, which are less and less labor-intensive and have been able to accumulate surplus, that we have been able to step back and see children as unique in themselves, as having an integrity of their own, and to look upon childhood as a period of active social growth, pleasurable and painful in itself. Gradually our laws have evolved to grant children more rights; to protect them from employers, abusive adults, and arranged marriages; and to guarantee them an education and security. In this process, we have begun to reconstruct parenting as a role chosen, not a duty, and child rearing as a process of challenge and self-actualization.

Moral Justifications of a Wanted Child

To say, then, that the ethics of a wanted child is a relatively new idea in history is not to dismiss those protectors of children who go back to ancient times. Rather it is to legitimate as a universal norm an idea of the child and childhood that has become part of the moral vision of modern societies. This ethic is based on three different ethical systems. First, from a utilitarian model, one that calculates costs and benefits, we know that wanted children contribute to the constructive (spiritual?) life of a community and do little to incur serious social costs. Second, from a Kantian perspective, the wanted child is valued for itself as a categorical imperative. However disappointed we may be with a particular child, the onus is on us to recall that children are valued for themselves as persons. Finally, and most important, the wanted child is at the center of a woman-based ethic. A wanted child is wanted by someone, and it is that person, the primary caregiver, who must reflect on the ethical choices and assume the responsibilities of parenting. The responsibility for raising children in our culture is parental. Fathers and mothers share this responsibility with each other and the community. In a patriarchal society, fathers have the authority. Their wives act on their instructions, and their children, like their wives, carry their names. In a more egalitarian model of the family, parenting is shared, although in the early years one parent plays a larger role than the other. Because the person playing the primary role is usually the mother or her surrogate, her position is privileged and her views have a status unlike that of the father or any of the elites—medical, religious, legal— who claim a unique status.

Within the pro-choice framework, the status of the fetus is unique, but the fetus is not a *person*. The fetus is considered to be a living and developing organism dependent for its life immediately on the woman carrying it. It is entitled to care and protection from environmental damage; its death comes with dignity and must not be the result of medical negligence or of violence. The fetus has, as Devine (1984) says, a moral claim on us but not enough of one for its death to bring a charge of feticide. Whether it is called subhuman, unborn, prehuman, potential person, or some other term is a question of semantics. Similarly, whether we describe an abortion as feticide, murder, termination of a pregnancy, incapacitating a fetus, or, as Bok (1984) has suggested, the withdrawal of a life-support system is a matter of semantics. Word games have become part of the politics of abortion. *Wholesale slaughter* and *genocide* are two of the more vivid and polemical terms used in an adversarial rhetoric; elective abortion, according to former Surgeon General C. Everett Koop, is "the slippery road that leads to Auschwitz."[43]

Language aside, what we can all agree on is that the fetus is amoral, without a moral capacity, incapable of doing good or evil, of being selfish or altruistic, of lying or telling the truth. Finally, the transition from being unborn to being born is qualitatively different from previous stages of development. Parturition marks a critical point in the biography of an individual; it is the moment of social membership into the family, community, culture, and, ultimately, history. Thus, the difference between unborn and born is *not* a slight developmental change, but an enormous existential one. It is greater than moving from one country to another, greater than a moral conversion, greater than even death and dying.

What divides the two positions, pro-life and pro-choice, then are, first, whether the emphasis is on the fetus as human life or on the neonate as person; and second, whether the emphasis is on the neonate as an individual with inherent rights or on reciprocal, inter-active relationships. Intellectually there is an impasse between the two paradigms, and it is not likely to be resolved by virtuoso feats of logic or science. The distinction between the two models is almost as old as consciousness itself and constitutes one of the archetypal tensions of the modern mind as each generation struggles with the competing claims of nature/nurture. The emphasis on fetal life, whether it comes from Catholicism or Protestantism, gives priority to a model of human behavior that is biologically determined; the emphasis on moral learning and social education gives priority to the historical and social world.

Summary

To summarize, the proponents of moral and religious opposition to abortion have their own version of the therapeutic abortion. To them, a therapeutic abortion is one that takes place before ensoulment, before that point in the process of gestation when the fetus or embryo acquires the special characteristics of being human and these characteristics begin to unfold. This definition coincides with medical opinion that an early abortion, one done in the first trimester, is safer and less traumatic than a later one. But the liberal position is canceled by a theory that humanness, however defined, begins at conception and that there is literally no period during the nine months when an abortion can be considered, regardless of how safe the procedure is or whether the reasons are serious or trivial.

Neither of these positions grants to the pregnant woman the right to engage in her own moral reasoning. Answers are given, delivered to her by moral elites who compete with medical and legal elites, and she is left to accept them uncritically and unconditionally. If she doesn't she faces condemnation. There is no educative or liberating experience in working through complicated moral decisions. No wonder, then, that a contemporary woman resents this method, for she is too well educated and is accustomed to more independence than these attitudes assume. She knows without being told that a decision made for her by others is not her decision and cannot be based on the same self-knowledge and nuance she has about herself. No matter whether it is a professor or a clergyman who tells you what to do, it is degrading to be told you lack the ability to think clearly about a decision that affects you. This can produce a kind of rebellion, alienation, or obstinacy that impedes intelligent decision making, for no one knows a woman's best interest better than she does.

Objecting to Abortion, or Who Decides?

There is no formal rational or ethical basis for rejecting either abortion or the right to choice. Yet, listening to the moral community presenting its case, it is sometimes difficult to know whether it objects more to abortion or the right to choice, to terminating fetal life or giving up the authority to make decisions of this nature. To the extent that mainstream religious leaders confront the medical and legal professions, they object to abortion; to the extent that they are confronting their own left, they object to delegating choice to the sinner.

This may explain why the questions asked by the layperson, male or female, have not been answered. Under what circumstances and for what reasons can we condone abortion? Or oppose it? The mainstream Church has left that question to the state. As an alternative, I have suggested, there is a dual ethic for abortion and choice. Both rest on the concept of the wanted child, which reflects a choice and a commitment. We cannot emphasize often enough that this is not an individualistic ethic, but a position that emphasizes relationships. The legal perspective that we turn to next has tried to balance the sacred and the secular, to resolve the conflict between "ought" and "is," by creating standards of conformity.

The Legal Model and Elective Abortion: Privacy

The pro-choice movement has never had any illusions that it could persuade pro-life supporters to reconsider and change their minds. True believers are not dissuaded by debating points, however well scored the debate may be. Instead, both sides have looked to legislatures and the courts for some final adjudication of the dispute. But here pro-life supporters are at a disadvantage, for the constitutional doctrine that separates church and state restrains the state from imposing on its citizens, who are of many religious backgrounds, a particular point of view. The strategy of the pro-life movement has been to build a broader, nondenominational base and to pressure state and federal legislators, saying it represents a moral community or, at least, a moral consensus.

Legislators and judges, although often sympathetic to pro-life advocates, have steadfastly refused to comment on when life beings, noting only that scientists are not agreed among themselves and that it is a question people trained in the law are not qualified to answer. The education, training, and experience of legislators and judges prepare them to discuss a much narrower part of the problem: rights.

Rights are not the equivalent of a moral conscience. The latter is broader and functions without external rewards and punishments. Conscientious objectors appeal to a higher law. Furthermore, in the liberal common-law tradition the term *rights* sounds more imperative than it is because rights are continually modified, revised, and redefined so as to become more or less congruent with changing social experience. But having rights, as such, is also part of that experience, so that changing them is also part of changing ourselves and the social institutions that exert such force on our lives.

Feminists and many other pro-choice advocates had hoped the courts would establish the fundamental right of a woman to make decisions about her own body; that is, to establish making the decision whether or not to terminate a pregnancy as a right similar to her right to vote. It was not an unreasonable expectation because, for the most part, women were already making those choices with great risks to themselves and without approval by the state. Their reasons were not to avoid personal inconvenience but to improve the quality of life for their families. In a country where there is no widespread practice of single mothers rearing children, the unmarried woman who opts for abortion believes she is being consistent with the values of the society. Similarly, in a country where economic security is correlated with education, the high-school girl who opts for abortion so she can remain in school and complete her education may be breaking one law but following another. Each case is different, but women expect to make this decision, just as they make other important decisions in their lives. These decisions are as rational as decisions can be in a society that sends out conflicting messages.

One of the baffling contradictions is the distinction made between the freedom to conceive children and the denial of the right to end pregnancies. If the state has a compelling interest, it surely should be in the birthrate, which has immediate repercussions for communities, educational systems, and the economy. Yet women do not need permission to have a child. It dismays but does not surprise us that in China the government actively discourages childbearing and rewards taking measures (the use of contraception, sterilization, late marriages) to prevent having children. American policies would seem very irrational to Chinese women, not because they are a reverse of their own government's position, but because the rewards and punishments are not balanced. There is something unusual and unexplained about the state's emphasizing a woman's freedom to procreate while withholding from her the freedom to decide not to carry a conceptus to term. Is there some vestigial fear of women's sexuality that lies behind this strange inversion of rules and refuses to let a woman make a crucial decision about her body and her social role? Do men think that once a fetus exists it belongs to them more than it belongs to the woman who carries it? These may be some of the deeper fears in the minds of legal scholars that inhibit their willingness to grant women what they regard as obvious: Pregnancy and the termination of pregnancy are all part of the same domain.

Law and the Right to Privacy

In the landmark cases, the courts did not deal with the right to choose but with the right to privacy. Feminists critical of the doctrine of privacy because it protects domestic wife abuse were dissatisfied with the court. However, for most women who distanced themselves from any larger doctrinaire position on abortion, women who took abortion literally and not symbolically, privacy, in its many meanings, was the issue (Allen 1988). Women, including many who have been badly abused in private by partners, feel the state has no right to dictate a decision as intimate as whether to bear a child or to impose a form of compulsory motherhood on a woman who has, for whatever reason, an unplanned pregnancy. Thus, in the two major decisions, *Griswold v. Connecticut* and *Roe v. Wade* (the first, brought in 1965 by the Directors of the Planned Parenthood League of Connecticut who had been arrested for providing a married couple with information on contraception, dealt with access to contraceptive information; the second, in 1973, was based on the refusal of Texas to allow a woman who had been gang-raped to procure an abortion), the courts spoke for mainstream America. Privacy in sexual and procreative matters is something American women have learned and value; the privacy of a sexual relationship between consenting adults has its own sanctity. We deplore invasions of privacy by the state, school, and social agency. Nothing reveals this so clearly as our automatic, conscious or unconscious, aversion to the population policies of contemporary China where the state is present in the bedroom of every couple during their childbearing years (Stacey 1983).

The Supreme Court held, however, that the right of privacy is not absolute or unlimited. In *Roe v. Wade* the Supreme Court declared that the privacy concepts in the Constitution applied only to the first trimester. After that, according to the decision, abortion must be thought of as a medical matter, and in the final trimester there must be evidence that the life of the mother is truly endangered. The Supreme Court, then, legitimated both elective *and* therapeutic abortion and, in addition, strengthened the legal position of the medical profession.

Because most abortions, approximately 90 percent, take place in the first trimester, it would seem almost academic to restrain abortions in the second and third trimester, especially because more abortions would occur earlier if access was improved. Why, then, did the Supreme Court limit the choice to the first trimester and not trust women in later stages? One possibility is that members of the court picture a fetus of six months to be more like ourselves than a fetus of one or two months. This vision, as has been suggested, results from the bias of our own imaginations encouraged by a nuclear family. What is being protected by the trimester distinction is a picture of something that looks like a person with five little fingers and five little toes, but still has a tail and is, from any other perspective, sociological or psychological, as distant from being a person as it was at an earlier stage. Without that visual depiction, there would be no reason for elective abortion to be unacceptable at any time. Nevertheless, *Roe v. Wade* laid a foundation for a concept of fetal rights in holding that there could be a conflict of interest in the later stages of the pregnancy.

Access and the Erosion of Privacy Rights

What the Supreme Court of the United States giveth, it can also take away. After having granted women the right to have elective abortions performed by licensed physicians, it made no provisions for women to have access to the services. Indeed, it opened the door to a backlash by Congress and state legislatures, which made abortion as difficult as possible. Women on welfare became the target of pro-life groups seeking to prevent the government from using Medicaid to pay for abortions. Why should the public be forced to pay for services that a significant minority find contrary to their religion? Is a hospital built with public funds but subsequently sold to private interests required to perform abortions? "The fact that a woman has a qualified right to an abortion," Robert Bork wrote, "does not imply a correlative right to free treatment."[44] President Carter told a press conference, "There are many things in life that are not fair, that wealthy people can afford and poor people can't. But I don't believe the federal government should take action to try to make these opportunities exactly equal, particularly when there is a moral factor involved." "The President has it backwards," the Rochester *Democrat and Chronicle* wrote. "It's precisely because there is a moral factor involved that the opportunities for elective abortion should be exactly equal. Otherwise Carter is guilty of legislating morality through economics: Using federal funds to subject the poor to more stringent moral requirements than the rich. That won't wash."[45]

The right of privacy, then, could be denied to the thirty percent of women whose abortions were funded by Medicaid. It could also be denied to women in the armed forces or whose husbands were in the services. The discriminatory implications of the ruling shocked all sorts of people who may have been lukewarm on the subject of abortion but were quick to recognize the social injustice of closing beds in municipal hospitals to poor women seeking abortions. Editorial opinion that was divided on *Roe v. Wade* instantly recognized the unfairness of the principle. "The right of privacy—or at least as it applies to poor people dependent on government assistance—has now been cast into the fires of public political dispute," according to *The Philadelphia Inquirer*.

Other kinds of restrictions have proliferated, including requirements to notify spouses, parents, and others, which serve no purpose except to humiliate the women. As the restrictions increase, so do the infrastructures required to enforce them, and the women involved are left to fall back on the neighborhood amateur paramedic. In short, a right is severely compromised if access does not complement it, and access, in turn, depends on physicians.

Physicians are not well known for their liberalism. In some cases, Catholic physicians feel enjoined by medical ethics to refer women to other physicians, but in small communities there may be no choice except to travel elsewhere. In general, doctors prefer legal abortions over illegal ones, but their first choice may be for adoption (Powell, Griffore, Kallen, and Popovich, 1991). Whether *Roe v. Wade* strengthened the power of the physicians as gatekeepers or failed to diminish what was already there is a matter of conjecture, but abortion in the years following the 1973 decision was far from being permissive.

The Myth of Fetal Rights

Fetal rights apparently begin in the second trimester. On that basis some of our contemporary legal scholars have created a courtroom drama of a tragic conflict between fetal rights (Hamlet?) and maternal rights (Gertrude?). Tribe (1990) sees this as "the clash of absolutes" that can only end in a compromise that is not satisfactory to either pro- or anti-choice groups. Glendon (1987) similarly constructs the situation so as to make a compromise seem inevitable.

Glendon argues that pro-choice supporters are forced to deny the strength of fetal rights because of the lack of any family policy in the United States compared with most of the developed countries of Europe. Discussions of divorce are similarly perverted by the dependency of children. If we had a generous set of family policies, there would be less demand for pro-choice.

What Glendon assumes is that abortion is part of family law and not a strategy for the empowerment of women who have been dependent. If we look at it as part of a historical trend toward self-direction and personal autonomy, the appropriate parallel is not with family law but with suffrage. Imagine telling women in the 1920s that there was a clash of absolutes between their right to vote and the right of the state to restrict voting to men only. Therefore, a compromise would have to be found. Perhaps women could vote in every other election.

Conflict as a Legal Fiction

The fallacy of Tribe's analysis and to some extent of Glendon's is to confuse the politics of abortion, the polarization of attitudes, with a genuine legal conflict. The truth is that it is a legal reflex to think in terms of conflict in which the courts arbitrate and out of these numerous arbitrations accumulate a set of precedents that become the legal culture. Typically, legal thinkers like Tribe believe the law can be fair and objective and that legal education trains professionals to think objectively. Thus, the myth of conflict gives to third parties an authority and credibility that partisans do not have.

Judges have even begun to want lawyers appointed to represent the interests of the fetus. What is insidious about this fiction that at some point we must choose between fetal rights and maternal rights is not the notion of fetal rights, but of maternal rights. The fiction assumes that a pregnant woman is a mother, not a woman who is deciding whether or not to become a mother. There is no conflict between fetal rights and maternal rights, although there may be a great deal of conflict in the woman's mind as she weighs the alternatives. But an abortion conducted in the later stages of pregnancy is not to save the life of the *mother* but the life of a *woman* who may also be a mother to previously born children as well as being a wage-earner, a member of a political party, and an active member of her church. It easier to mobilize sentiment for the woman around the role of motherhood than around the role of teacher, but to assume that a pregnant woman is a mother by definition is to preempt her own rationality. The real decision a woman may be making is between fetal rights and the rights of an older member of the family who needs full-time help, or between fetal rights and the rights of a husband with a heart condition. As weighed against these other rights, the fetal right is not only second, it also has a qualitatively different claim on her.

As we have seen earlier, the concept of fetal rights has been used not to save the life of the fetus or of the woman carrying it, but to label women as unfit mothers and to justify removing a newborn from the woman who has just gone through 18 hours of labor to deliver it. Thus, the state's compelling interest is not in the fetal life but in controlling the life-styles of women in a patriarchal society. The alternative is to locate the state's compelling interest in the relationships of infants to their care-givers, to ensure that these are conducive to health and social well-being.

Bodily Integrity

Many legal scholars and others have debated the question of abortion around the idea that a woman has or does not have the right to control her own body. Because a pregnancy is so palpably a body within a body, we are inclined to argue that body integrity is at stake in the abortion decision. Hence, the emphasis on a mother's life. But the body and mind are not distinct; they form an interactive whole. To deprive women of the right to make up their own minds about abortion is to deprive them of the integrity of their minds as well as of their bodies. An enforced pregnancy is not just a strain on the body. It demeans the whole relationship of a woman to herself; it devalues her. We know from cases of false pregnancy that pregnancy is a mental, a psychosomatic phenomenon that is denied in the exclusive emphasis on body integrity. In her analysis of abortion, Judith Jarvis (1979) asks us to consider what would happen if we woke up one morning chained to a famous violinist who needed our kidney for a period of nine months. Her analysis focuses on the encroachment on body integrity. What we are suggesting here is that a woman deprived of choice is made dependent on a social structure. It is not the cosmetics aspects of an unplanned, unwanted pregnancy that are devastating; it is the social and psychological aspects that devalue all women. The right to life she wants is physical and emotional security. There are not too many cases, these days, when a woman's life is threatened by a pregnancy, but there are many where a woman's self-respect is threatened and a growing number where she must consider fetal surgery. If she cannot be compelled to allow fetal surgery, it is not because the state cannot compel her to undergo surgery, but because the state cannot compel her to surrender a decision that is inherently hers.

Do We Need a Law?

Americans are surprised to learn that at present Canada has no abortion law. Since 1988 when the Canadian Supreme Court held that section 251 of the Criminal Code was contrary to Section 7 of the Charter of Rights and Freedoms, the country has been without a law, a condition that spokespersons for the government refer to as a vacuum (*Morgentaler v. The Queen*).[46] In the spring of 1990 a moderate bill, introduced into Parliament and passed by the House of Commons by seven votes, failed in the Senate; following that defeat the Minister of Justice announced there were no plans to introduce new legislation. Since then, in a case involving two midwives, the Supreme Court of Canada declared the fetus did not have rights as a person under the Criminal Code until it was fully born. Thus far the sky has not fallen and the social fabric has not unravelled, despite dire predictions by anti-choice groups who have kept up steady pressure on doctors and hospitals who perform abortions to refrain from doing so, on doctors to stop opening up new clinics, and on the Provinces to exclude payments for abortions under Medicare. On the local level they have tried to have sex education taken out of the schools, and on the national level they are attempting to prevent the use of RU-486.

Politics aside, what the Canadian experience demonstrates is that the legal debates about abortion may be of less significance than lawyers would like to believe. To the pro-life movement in Canada, the absence of a law is itself a form of legal injustice; to the pro-choice movement, no law may be a lesser form of legal injustice than laws that are patently unjust. Neither side is naive enough to accept the myth of legal theorists that law transcends social conflict. It only transcends the conflicts that they themselves recognize and define.

To summarize, in 1973 when the Supreme Court of the United States held that the Texas law denying a woman an abortion was unconstitutional, it ended an era of Victorian morality and hypocrisy by recognizing abortion as a reality for many women. It acknowledged a woman's right to privacy, but did not affirm the principle of the wanted child.

By the time of the court's *Roe v. Wade* decision, a younger, more liberal generation of lawyers was moving in the same direction, pleading for compromise. Implicit in their model of compromise is the assumption that the state has a mediating role to play in conflict and it is evident that the state is unable to perform this function unless there is a large cadre of neutrals who are trained in mediation skills and understand both sides. It is the professional hubris of lawyers to think they are neutral and the law they represent is objective. If that were the case we would have far more distributive justice in our society than we presently have, and that situation might do more than the laws and regulations to reduce the rates of abortion.

Who Benefits from Unenforceable Laws?

Unenforceable laws have social costs. Political order depends on a legal system that citizens can live with, comply with, and defend. Hence, when women have abortions despite the law, the social order itself is subverted. The family is also harmed. Whenever the life and health of women is threatened, whenever illegal abortions and illegal contraception lead to complications for future fertility, the family as an institution is endangered.

Finally, the post *Roe v. Wade* legislation that has allowed states to erode the decision by discriminating against the poor, against youth, and against women shows the extent to which laws and legal decisions about abortion are, indirectly, a form of social legislation, a constituent of the welfare state. The enemies of the welfare state have displaced onto women much of their anger about social legislation. This would explain why opposition to abortion is part of a more general conservative coalition.

Chapter 5

Pro-Choice as the Alternative

Language

A shudder runs through the American psyche when the phrase *abortion on demand* is mentioned. These dreaded words conjure up some apocalyptic vision of a nation where citizens accustomed to practicing contraception suddenly stop, where women in various stages of pregnancy line up in long queues around hospitals and clinics to undergo a procedure painful enough to require a local anesthetic and wearing enough to call for a few days of bed rest. An unlikely scenario, but it illustrates how powerful words are and the extent to which they elicit an over-reaction. The more descriptive empirical approach pursued here provides us with a reality unobscured by the heat of impassioned rhetoric.

We have purposely not dealt with the activities of social movements although, as we have suggested, abortion is a political issue. But analyzing the formation of pro-life and pro-choice groups and the tactics they have used on the streets, in the courtrooms, and in the lobbying of state and federal representatives is best left to the social historians. Instead, we chose to look mainly at the ideas and the logic and value systems embedded in them, testing these ideas against the reality of the abortion experience.

Does Elective Abortion Go Far Enough?

What emerged as we looked at abortion in different historical contexts and in the special case of teenagers is that elective abortion is an essential

135

aspect of family planning, and that family planning is the foundation of the modern family-centered ethic of a wanted child. The distinction between contraception and abortion makes no sense to women in whose minds they are linked and are back-up for each other. Some women prefer contraception but find it difficult; others simply prefer abortion. The distinction between contraception and abortion, between proactive and reactive methods, has become more ambiguous with the new oral steroid drug RU-486, sometimes called the abortion pill.

RU-486 (mifepristone) induces menses and appears to have no iatrogenic side effects (Silvestre et al. 1990). Because it is not technically an abortifacient, it avoids the criticism of abortion as destroying a life, and because it is nonsurgical (it is taken in tablet form and followed up, within 48 hours, by an injection or suppository of prostaglandin) the risks of infection and other problems are eliminated. In addition, both the psychological and economic costs of more invasive methods are reduced. But its effectiveness is limited to the first six or seven weeks of a pregnancy, so that it is not available to women with more advanced pregnancies.

RU-486 is one piece in the larger, more humanistic set of assumptions about the family and society, assumptions that are abbreviated in the phrase *Every child a wanted child.* Every unwanted child is a reproach. Poverty and racism are also a reproach, and we cannot assume that every abortion represents an unwanted child. More black women than white disapprove of abortion (McCormick 1975), yet more black women than white have abortions. More black women than white have illegal abortions, and more black women than white die of illegal abortions. These four sets of data frame a social tragedy around abortion that is lost in the abstruse, erudite philosophical and legal discussions of abortion. It is useless to talk about the ethics of the wanted child without talking about the ethics of poverty, racism, hospital gatekeeping, and access to medical services.

Nor is it possible to talk about the ethics of the wanted child without talking about gender inequality. Because we have no way of measuring the frequency of unplanned pregnancies that are nonconsensual we can only conjecture that it is high. It is clearly the case, as we saw, with the teenager who is more prone to talk about it, but we do not know how many older women have nonconsensual intercourse or nonconsensual pregnancies. Until we have symmetrical gender roles, the abortion option is at worst a reluctant choice for women who would have liked a child; at best, compensatory justice for those who are pregnant against their own will.

I do not want to dwell here on the inadequacies of the pro-life ideology that looks at reproduction through the eyes of men (celibate men, at that, in the case of priests) and punishes women for the sexual permissiveness of men. The most recent illustration of the cruelty of anti-abortion policies comes from Romania where in 1975 the government repealed all laws permitting abortion and contraception and made abortion a criminal offense punishable by death. What was intended as a deterrent became a misogynist massacre, for during the decade of the 1980s, Romania had a higher abortion rate and more abortion-related maternal deaths than any other European country (Jacobson 1990). The unnecessary deaths of women caused by Draconian legislation is truly murder.

American society is more humane, but it is not neutral. We continue to make women feel guilty about abortion by using a discourse that creates the myth of fetal life and by fostering a modern obstetrical practice that encourages prenatal bonding. As we have suggested here, the way we think about the fetus and the way we picture it in our imaginations or depict it in medical textbooks are related to a prior family system that regards children as family property. Elsewhere, in societies where adoption is more common and the nuclear family is not the only or dominant model, the fetus is drawn differently, in a more impersonal way, and the psychological attachment to it is more perfunctory. Women in these situations have abortions with as little compunction as we have about contraception. In American society we have normalized contraception but continue to regard abortion as abnormal, a special case that could have been avoided. Yet it should be clear by now that if abortion is to have the same status as contraception we must stop sentimentalizing the fetus by reading into it a version of childhood and child development and by retroactively endowing it with social intelligence as if the womb was a Rorschach card onto which we projected our own wishes.

Children's Rights Are Not Fetal Rights

The fetus is a signal to a woman who must ask if this is a wanted child. The child acquires legal rights with birth and starts life in the environment of the delivery room when the umbilical cord is tied and survival becomes dependent on the quality of relationships between the infant and persons in its social space. The type of nurturing, the physical and emotional security, the educational stimulation given to children in infancy and youth shape their personalities, character, ambitions, and emotional resources. The experience of parenting affects us and modifies our understanding of the legitimate moral claims a child may make. Children's rights, one of the newer areas of legal analysis, constitutes one measure of the morality of a nation. It is understandable that in our enthusiasm for children's rights we want to extend them retrospectively to the fetus, but the idea of fetal rights is only a metaphor for the rights of children that begin at birth. Similarly, the only significant bondings for a child's development are the relationships in the early life of the child when we establish the potentiality of the child. Again, to read potential and potentiality into a fetus is a literary device, a form of selective embryology, not a fact.

Only socialized persons can become more than they are, can stretch their limitations through creative effort, and that, in turn, requires a great deal of opportunity, encouragement, and feedback from our social institutions. It is worth pointing out that a society which says it values the family is deceiving itself if its institutions favor some children over others on an arbitrary, ascriptive basis. Children soon learn it is one thing to be a wanted child at home and another to be an unwanted child in the neighborhood and classroom.

Our society, like most, has its gender preferences. Although we do not practice female infanticide or deprive girls of care and education, our larger social structures withhold from women the same kinds of opportunity and autonomy they afford men. The most common rationalization for this is biology, which attributes the differences between male and female to the reproductive systems of women. Pregnancy becomes an illness requiring medical services. Women who are between pregnancies are subject to mood swings and chronic premenstrual syndrome that may require medical or psychiatric services. Menopausal women are prone to depressive disorders. This list is a slight exaggeration, but it illustrates how gender differences are reduced to biology and how reproduction becomes a lifetime disability.

The feminist movement, throughout its history, has argued against biological determinism and the particular construction of reproductive functions. Characteristics described as natural are shown to be culturally specific, whereas dependency can be understood as the result of inequality, not its cause. Much of the attention has been given to the medical establishment, which became almost the prototype of patriarchy from the recruitment and education of doctors to high-tech, hospital-centered childbirth. In response, the women's movement promoted the demedicalization of reproduction through home births and greater use of midwives. Women also began to question why so many pregnancies were labeled *high risk* and whether the tests and chemical medications used exacerbated the risks.

The same critical thinking and philosophy was applied to abortion. It, too, could be demystified and demedicalized; it, too, could be done outside the environment of hospitals. The therapeutic abortion, which depends on the approval of licensed medical practitioners, was the equivalent of the high-risk pregnancy. This is not to suggest that we can totally demedicalize childbirth or abortion, but rather to illuminate the counter-trend that attempts to liberate women from the fortunes of the pharmaceutical industries, from the careerism of obstetrical specialists, and from the impersonal bureaucratic structures of hospitals. Other dissident groups were also discovering non–Western medicine, more natural methods of relieving pain (biomedical feedback, for example), and other ways of organizing the delivery of health services. The older model in which the professional is an autocrat could be replaced by one in which the professional is a coordinator, some of whose duties could be delegated to nurse practitioners, lay healers, and others outside the system.

Pro-choice as a Political Choice

The evaluation of these trends will come much later. My point here is to note that the feminist pro-choice position is not just about abortion and wanted children; it is a critique of a system. An elective abortion means something more than privacy and access to services, something more than compensatory justice or answering a social need. It is related to a larger strategy of social change, of gender and justice. *Roe v. Wade* was an important step in furthering a child-centered family, in giving women a voice to decide on one of the most crucial events in their lives. But abortion rights, as distinct from the availability of elective abortion, are a political issue closely related to patients' rights movements and are not unlike the struggle for political rights. Like the suffrage issue, abortion rights are both means and ends, they are transformative and empower women to act as agents of social change. The two, elective abortion and abortion rights, may overlap, and women may make, as I have attempted to do here, both cases in contrast to pro-life with its implacable opposition to either abortion rights or elective abortion. But most men, most middle-of-the-roaders, can probably live with elective abortion, which extends more freedom to women but leaves the status quo (a system of gender, race, and class inequality) intact. What is threatening is the radical message in abortion rights that empowers women and, in doing so, undermines a gender-based power structure. Thus, one finds in the pro-choice movement many women who do not have children by choice or who are beyond childbearing years. In the last analysis, then, this hidden agenda may account for the extraordinary efforts to erode *Roe v. Wade*. Pro-life advocates, like Operation Rescue and the Mormon Church, are merely the shock troops of a conservative stand against any changes in a system of male paternalism and gender privilege. Abortion is the tip of the iceberg.

Beyond American Pragmatism and Toward a New Ethic

Modern history is on the side of equality and liberation; the best traditions of the American experience extend choice to ordinary citizens and place confidence in the judgments of those groups most affected. The roots of pro-choice are in the American experience; the roots of pro-life are in the feudal world. But if the question of abortion is to be resolved creatively, we have to go beyond the middle-class pragmatism of the American experience and the moral dogmatism of the feudal world in developing a new ethical model that oppresses neither woman nor child.

Notes

Chapter 1. Introduction

1. Ely Van De Warker, M.D. *The Detection of Criminal Abortion and a Study of Foeticidal Drugs* (Boston: James Campbell, 1972) reprinted in *Abortion in Nineteenth-Century America* (New York: Arno Press. 1974), 7.

2. Susan T. Foh, "Abortion and Women's Lib," in *Thou Shall Not Kill,* ed. Richard L. Ganz (New Rochelle, NY: Arlington House, 1978), 161.

3. Linda Bird Franckc, *The Ambivalence of Abortion* (New York: Random House, 1978), 64.

4. John Hudgins, "Is Birth Control Genocide?" *The Black Scholar,* Nov.–Dec. 1972: 34–37.

5. Cited by Henry P. David in "Abortion Research in Transnational Perspective: An Overview," in *Abortion Research: International Experience,* ed. Henry P. David (Lexington, MA: Lexington Books, 1974), 7.

6. Francke, 185.

7. Mary K. Zimmerman, *Passage Through Abortion* (New York: Praeger, 1977), 143.

8. Quoted in E. Patricia McCormick, *Attitudes Toward Abortion* (Lexington, MA: Lexington Books, 1975), 105.

9. Ibid., 107.

10. Government of Canada, *Report of the Committee on the Operation of the Abortion Law* (Ottawa, 1977), 195.

11. Francke, 190.

12. Zimmerman, 142.

13. Statement by NancyJo Mann in David C. Reardon, *Aborted Women Silent No More* (Chicago: Loyola University Press, 1987), x.

14. McCormick, 105.

15. In England abortion legislation was recently liberalized, allowing a broader basis for abortions, but stricter limitations were put on embryo research.

16. Government of Canada, *Report of Committee on the Operation of the Abortion Law* (Ottawa, 1977), 193.

17. Government of Canada, *Report of Committee on the Operation of the Abortion Law* (Ottawa, 1977), 199.

Chapter 2. Comparative Models

18. Maguire, Daniel C. 1984. *Reflections of a Catholic Theologian on Visiting an Abortion Clinic.* Catholics for a Free Choice. Washington, D.C., no page indicated.

19. Government of Canada, *Report on the Operation of the Abortion Law* (Ottawa, 1977), 197.

20. Beryl Rowland, trans., *Medieval Woman's Guide to Health* (Kent, OH: Kent State University Press, 1981), 97.

21. Kristin Luker, *Abortion and the Politics of Motherhood* (Berkeley: University of California Press, 1984), 15.

22. Nanette J. Davis, *From Crime to Choice* (Westport, CT: Greenwood Press, 1985), 44.

23. Raymond Illsely and Marion Hall, "Psychsocial Research in Abortion: Selected Issues," in *Abortion in Psychosocial Perspective,* eds. Henry P. David et al. (New York: Springer), 12.

Chapter 3. Teenage Pregnancy: The Double Standard and the Limitations of Contraception

24. Government of Canada, *Report on the Operation of the Abortion Law* (Ottawa, 1977), 198.

25. Zimmerman, Mary K., *Passage through Abortion* (New York: Praeger, 1977), 140.

26. Ganz, 30.

27. Tomas Silber, M.D., "Abortion in Adolescence: The Ethical Dimension," *Adolescence,* XV, no. 464–74.

28. McCormick, 101–2.

29. Joffe, Carol, *The Regulation of Sexuality* (Philadelphia: Temple University Press, 1986), 120.

30. Bernard Häring, "A Theological Evaluation," in *The Morality of Abolition,* ed. John T. Noonan, Jr. (Cambridge, MA: Harvard University Press, 1970), 141.

Chapter 4. Three Patterns of Discourse

31. "Criminal Abortion: Its Extent and Prevention," paper read by Dr. Andrew Nebinger to the Philadelphia County Medical Society, February 9, 1870, 5. Reprinted in *Abortion in Nineteenth-Century America,* eds. Charles Rosenberg and Carroll Smith-Rosenberg (New York: Arno Press, 1974).

32. Government of Canada, *Report on the Operation of the Abortion Law* (Ottawa, 1977), 193.

33. Nathanson, Bernard D., M.D., *The Abortion Papers Inside the Abortion Mentality* (New York: Frederick Fell, 1983), 4.

34. Stephen D. Schwarz, *The Moral Question of Abortion,* (Chicago: Loyola Press, 1990), 17.

35. John F. Frame, "Abortion from a Biblical Perspective," in *Thou Shall Not Kill,* ed. Richard L. Ganz (New Rochelle, NY: Arlington House, 1978), 70.

36. Beverly Wildung Harrison, *Our Right to Choose. Toward a New Ethic of Abortion* (Boston: Beacon, 1983), 131.

37. McCormick, 110.

38. Frame, 45.

39. Paul D. Ramsey, "The Morality of Abortion," in *Life or Death: Ethics and Options,* eds. Edward Shils et al. (1968), 60–93.

40. John T. Noonan, Jr., "An Almost Absolute Value in History," in *The Problem of Abortion,* ed. Joel Feinberg (Belmont, CA: Wadsworth, 1984), 13.

41. Tristram H. Englehardt, Jr., "Introduction," in *Abortion and the Status of the Fetus,* eds. William B. Bondeson et al. (Dordrecht, Holland: R. Reidel Publishing Co., 1983), xv.

42. Feinberg, 135.

43. Koop, 23.

44. Bork, Robert. Quoted in editorial in *Manchester Union Leader,* Manchester, New Hampshire, April 4, 1976. The quote is from a brief filed in the Supreme Court on a Pennsylvania appeal. See Lauren R. Sass, *Abortion: Freedom of Choice & the Right to Life.* (New York: Facts on File).

45. Rochester, New York. *Democrat and Chronicle.* July 16, 1977.

46. Section 251 of the Criminal Code was as follows: "Every one who, with intent to procure the miscarriage of a female person, whether or not she is pregnant, uses any means for the purpose of carrying out his intention is guilty of an indictable offence and is liable to imprisonment for life."

Bibliography

Adler, Nancy E., and Peggy Dolcini. 1986. "Psychological Issues in Abortion for Adolescents." In *Adolescent Abortion. Psychological and Legal Issues*, edited by Gary B. Melton. Lincoln: University of Nebraska Press.

Allen, Anita L. 1988. *Uneasy Access*. Totowa, N.J.: Rowman & Littlefield.

Blake, Judith. 1973. "Elective Abortion and our Reluctant Citizenry: Research on Public Opinion in the United States." In *The Abortion Experience*, edited by Howard J. Osofsky and Joy D. Osofsky, 447–67. New York: Harper and Row.

Bok, Sissela. 1984. "Ethical Problems of Abortion." In *The Problem of Abortion*, edited by Joel Feinberg. Belmont, CA: Wadsworth Publishing Co.

Bonavoglia, Angela. 1990. "Kathy's Day in Court." In *From Abortion to Reproductive Freedom*, edited by Marlene Gerber Fried. Boston: South End Press.

Borg, Susan, and Judith Lasker. 1982. *When Pregnancy Fails*. London: Routledge & Kegan Paul.

Cates, Willard, Jr., and David A. Grimes. 1981. "Morbidity and Mortality of Abortion in the United States." In *Abortion and Sterilization: Medical and Social Aspects*, edited by Jane E. Hodgson. London: Academic Press.

David, Henry P., ed. 1974. *Abortion Research: International Experience*. Lexington, MA: Lexington Books.

David, Henry P., and Herbert L. Friedman. 1973. "Psychosocial Research in Abortion: A Transnational Perspective." In *The Abortion Experience. Psychological & Medical Impact*, edited by Howard J. Osofsky and Joy D. Osofsky, 310–37. New York: Harper and Row.

Davis, Angela Y. 1983. *Women, Race & Class*. New York: Vintage.

Davis, Nanette J. 1985. *From Crime to Choice*. Westport, CT: Greenwood Press.

Devereux, George. 1960. *A Study of Abortion in Primitive Societies*. London: Thomas Yoseloff Ltd.

Devine, Philip. 1984. "The Scope of the Prohibition Against Killing." In *The Problem of Abortion*, edited by Joel Feinberg. Belmont, CA: Wadsworth.

Doncel, Joseph, S. J. 1984. "A Liberal Catholic's View." In *The Problem of Abortion*, edited by Joel Steinberg. Belmont, CA: Wadsworth.

Engelhardt, Tristram H., Jr. 1983. "Introduction." In *Abortion and the Status of the Fetus*, edited by William B. Bondeson, Tristram H. Engelhardt, Jr., Stuart F. Spicker, and Daniel H. Winship. Dordrecht, Holland: R. Reidel Publishing Co.

Fallaci, Oriana. 1975. *Letter to a Child Never Born*, trans. by John Shepley. New York: Pocket Books, Washington Square Press.

Farber, Naomi. 1990. "The Significance of Race and Class in Marital Decisions among Unmarried Adolescent Mothers." *Social Problems*, 37, no. 1: 51–63.

Feinberg, Joel, The Problem of Abortion (Belmont, CA: Wadsworth, 1984).

Fletcher, John C., and Mark I. Evans. 1983. "Maternal Bonding in Early Fetal Ultrasound Examinations," *The New England Journal of Medicine*, vol. 308–309: 392–93.

Frame, John F. 1978. "Abortion from a Biblical Perspective." In *Thou Shalt Not Kill*, edited by Richard L. Ganz. New Rochelle, NY: Arlington House.

Francke, Linda Bird. 1978. *The Ambivalence of Abortion*. New York: Random House.

Fujita, Byron N., and Nathaniel N. Wagner. 1973. "Referendum 20—Abortion Reform in Washington State." In *The Abortion Experience*, edited by Howard J. Osofsky and Joy D. Osofsky, 232–60. New York: Harper and Row.

Glendon, Mary Ann. 1987. *Abortion and Divorce in Western Law*. Cambridge, MA: Harvard University Press.

Gordon, Linda. 1976. *Woman's Body, Woman's Right*. New York: Penguin.

Greenglass, Esther. 1976. *After Abortion*. Toronto: Longman Canada.

Gustafson, James M. 1970. "A Protestant Ethical Approach." In *The Morality of Abortion*, edited by John T. Noonan, Jr. Cambridge MA: Harvard University Press.

Häring, Bernard. 1970. "A Theological Evaluation." In *The Morality of Abortion*, edited by John T. Noonan, Jr. Cambridge, MA: Harvard University Press.

Harris, Marvin, and Eric B. Ross. 1987. *Death, Sex, and Fertility*. New York: Columbia University Press.

Heitlinger, Alena. 1987. *Reproduction, Medicine & the Socialist State*. New York: St. Martin's Press.

Honig, Y., N. Dorshave, H. Zakut, and D. M. Serr. 1975. "Personality Characteristics and Attitudes towards Pregnancy and Motherhood in Women with Repeated Abortions." In *The Family*, edited by Herman Hirsch, M.D., 306–10. 4th International Congress of Psychosomatic Obstetrics and Gynecology. Basel: S. Karger.

Jacobson, Jodi L. 1990. *The Global Politics of Abortion*. World Watch Paper 97. Washington, DC: Worldwatch Institute.

Jane. 1990. "Just Call 'Jane'." In *From Abortion to Reproductive Freedom*, edited by Marlene Gerber Fried, 93–100. Boston: South End Press.

Jarvis, Judith. 1979. "A Defense of Abortion." In *Philosophy and Woman*, edited by Sharon Bishop and Marjorie Weinzweig. Belmont, CA: Wadsworth Publishing Company.

Joffe, Carol. 1986. *The Regulation of Sexuality*. Philadelphia: Temple University Press.

Jones, Elise F. et al. 1986. *Teenage Pregnancy in Industrialized Countries*. New Haven CT: Yale University Press.

Jones, Elise F., and Charles F. Westoff. 1973. "Changes in Attitudes Toward Abortion: With Emphasis Upon the National Fertility Study Data." In *The Abortion Experience*, edited by Howard J. Osofsky and Joy D. Osofsky, 468–81. New York: Harper and Row.

Kapor-Stanulovic, Nila and Herbert L. Friedman. 1978. "Studies in Choice Behavior in Yugoslavia." In *Abortion in Psychosocial Perspective*, edited by Henry P. David, et al., 119–44. New York: Springer.

Luker, Kristin. 1984. *Abortion and the Politics of Motherhood*. Berkeley: University of California Press.

Martire, Greg. n.d.g. "Polling Catholics on Abortion." In *The Abortion Issue in the Political Process*. Washington, DC: Catholics for a Free Choice.

McCartney, James J. 1987. *Unborn Persons. Pope John Paul II and the Abortion Debate*. New York: Peter Lang.

McCormack, Thelma. 1990. "'If Mama Boozes—Baby Loses.' The Fetal Alcohol Syndrome." Paper given Annual Meeting of Canadian Sociology and Anthropology Society, Victoria, B.C.

McCormick, E. Patricia. 1975. *Attitudes Toward Abortion*. Lexington, MA: Lexington.

McLaren, Angus, and Arlene Tigar McLaren. 1986. *The Bedroom and the State*. Toronto: McClelland and Stewart.

Melton, Gary B., ed. 1986. *Adolescent Abortion. Psychological and Legal Issues*. Lincoln: University of Nebraska Press.

Miller, Barbara D. 1981. *The Endangered Sex*. Ithaca, NY: Cornell University Press.

Mohr, James C. 1984. "Patterns of Abortion and the Response of American Physicians, 1790–1930." In *Women and Health in America*, edited by Judith Walzer Leavitt, 117–23. Madison: University of Wisconsin Press.

Dr. Henry Morgentaler, Dr. Leslie Frank Smolling v. Her Majesty the Queen and the Attorney General of Canada. Supreme Court of Canada. January 1988.

Nathanson, Bernard N., M.D., 1983. *The Abortion Papers: Inside the Abortion Mentality* (New York: Frederick Fell).

Noonan, John T., Jr. 1984. "An Almost Absolute Value in History." In *The Problem of Abortion*, edited by Joel Feinberg. Belmont, CA: Wadsworth Publishing Co.

Ooms, Theodora. 1984. "The Family Perspective on Abortion." In *Abortion. Understanding the Differences*, edited by Sidney Callahan and Daniel Callahan, 81–107. New York: Plenum.

Petchesky, Rosalind Pollack. 1985. *Abortion and Woman's Choice*. Boston: Northeastern University Press.

Pomeroy, Richard, and Lynn C. Landman. 1973. "American Public Opinion and Abortion in the Early Seventies." In *The Abortion Experience*, edited by Howard J. Osofsky and Joy D. Osofsky, 482–95. New York: Harper and Row.

Powell, Virginia, Robert J. Griffore, David J. Kallen, and Susan N. Popovich. 1991. "Physicians' Preferences for Adoption, Abortion, and Keeping a Child Among Adolescents." In *Research in the Sociology of Health Care*, vol. 9, edited by Dorothy Wertz, 33–47. Greenwich, CT: JAI Press.

Reardon, David C. 1987. *Aborted Women, Silent No More*. Chicago: Loyala University Press.

Resnick, Michael D. 1984. "Studying Adolescent Mothers' Decision Making about Adoption and Parenting," *Social Work*, January/February: 5–10.

Rodman, Hyman, Betty Sarvis and Joy Walker Bonar. 1987. *The Abortion Question* (New York: Columbia University Press).

Rosenberg, Charles, and Carroll Smith-Rosenberg, eds. 1974. *Abortion in Nineteenth-Century America*. New York: Arno Press.

Rowland, Beryl. 1981. *Medieval Woman's Guide to Health*. Kent, OH: Kent State University Press.

Ruddick, William. 1988. "Are Fetuses Becoming Children?" In *Ethics and Fetal Therapy*, edited by Carl Nimrod and Glenn Griener. Calgary, Alberta: Calgary Institute for the Humanities.

Schwarz, Stephen D. 1990. *The Moral Question of Abortion*. Chicago: Loyola Press.

Silber, Tomas, M.D. 1990. "Abortion in Adolescence: The Ethical Dimension," *Adolescence*. XV, no. 58: 464–74.

Silvestre, Louise M.D. et al. 1990. "Voluntary Interruption of Pregnancy with Mifepristone (RU486) and a Prostaglandin Analogue," *New England Journal of Medicine*, 332, no. 10. 645–648.

Stacey, Judith. 1983. *Patriarchy and Socialist Revolution in China*. Berkeley: University of California Press.

Stotland, Nada Logan, M.D. 1988. *Social Change and Women's Reproductive Health Care*. New York: Praeger.

Tietze, Christopher M.D., and Sarah Lewit. 1973. "A National Medical Experience: The Joint Program for the Study of Abortion (JPSA)." In *The Abortion Experience*, edited by Howard J. Osofsky and Joy D. Osofsky, 1–28. New York: Harper and Row.

Tribe, Lawrence. 1990. *Abortion the Clash of Absolutes*. New York: W. W. Norton.

Wertheimer, Roger. 1984. "Understanding the Abortion Argument." In *The Problem of Abortion*, edited by Joel Feinberg, 43–57. Belmont, CA: Wadsworth.

Williams, George Huntston. 1970. "The Sacred Condominium" in John T. Noonan,

Jr. (ed.) *The Morality of Abortion* (Cambridge, Mass.: Harvard University Press), 146–171.

Wright, Nathan. 1969. "Black Power vs. Black Genocide," *The Black Scholar*, Dec. 1969: 47–52.

Zelizer, Viviana A. 1985. *Pricing the Priceless Child*. New York: Basic.

Zimmerman, Mary K. 1977. *Passage Through Abortion*. New York: Praeger.